A Magnificent Work

"Daniel Oudshoorn is not a typical writer, but he is very good at telling you the story you need to hear. In his new book, *A Magnificent Work*, his truths cut like a knife, while at the same time, his insight and wisdom offer the kind of hope and healing he has seen in his own life and as learned wisdom he offers to society. You will not regret taking the time to hear *A Magnificent Work* speak to your own heart and mind, but you will be changed by it."

—**RANDY WOODLEY**
Author, activist, farmer, Eloheh Indigenous Center for Earth Justice

"Oudshoorn's prose is relentless. He deftly weaves lived experience with poignant social commentary to produce a text that is both deeply personal and universally relevant. His insight is striking, and he incites grief, rage, and hope while contextualizing these emotions within broader patterns of inequality. Evocative and timely, *A Magnificent Work* is a painfully necessary read."

—**NICOLE LUONGO**
Professor of Sociology, Keyano College

"Dan is generous in his vulnerability, sharing with the reader his inner self and hard thoughts in such a way that readers willingly travel with him on a tough yet enlightening trip. *A Magnificent Work* is extremely moving and demonstrates the deep-rooted connection between the well-being of self, community, and the environment. A read that opens up an invitation to have a fresh perspective on your own life and new awareness of the vital importance of the life around you."

—**JULIE BAUMANN**
Executive Director, SafeSpace London

"This book could have been called 'the sins of the fathers'; it is hard to read, but for some of us, necessary. Dancing between autobiography, national history, and geological time, Oudshoorn calls out the brutal patterns that link sexual violence, racist colonial violence, and ecocide. Starting from his own place of damage and complicity he stumbles towards a traitorous white masculinity, one that gets schooled, de-centers itself, and knows the cost of seeking to serve tenderness."

—**LAUREL DYKSTRA**
Priest of Salal + Cedar Watershed Discipleship Community,
Coast Salish Territory, British Columbia

A Magnificent Work

Daniel Oudshoorn

RESOURCE *Publications* · Eugene, Oregon

A MAGNIFICENT WORK

Copyright © 2020 Daniel Oudshoorn. All rights reserved. Except for brief quotations in critical publications or reviews, no part of this book may be reproduced in any manner without prior written permission from the publisher. Write: Permissions, Wipf and Stock Publishers, 199 W. 8th Ave., Suite 3, Eugene, OR 97401.

Resource Publications
An Imprint of Wipf and Stock Publishers
199 W. 8th Ave., Suite 3
Eugene, OR 97401

www.wipfandstock.com

PAPERBACK ISBN: 978-1-7252-6611-7
HARDCOVER ISBN: 978-1-7252-6612-4
EBOOK ISBN: 978-1-7252-6613-1

Manufactured in the U.S.A.   06/10/20

for Isaiah Antone, Roy Wilson, Jesse Debo, and Frank Winnie
because they burned that fucker down
and also and always and forever for
CBRM and RVBM and Jessica

"With this knife, O Earthman, I, Queen of the Banana, will cut you in pieces."[1]

1. Karapanou, *Kassandra and the Wolf*, 17.

Contents

The First Part: Son | 1
The Second Part: Father | 51
The Third Part: Fatherland | 103
The Fourth Part: Land | 143

Bibliography | 185

The First Part

Son

"And where, I ask you, can a man escape to, when he hasn't enough madness left inside him? The truth is an endless death agony. The truth is death. You have to choose: death or lies. I've never been able to kill myself."[1]

---

1. Céline, *Journey to the End of the Night*, 173.

1

My father, in his own defense, often said that although he may not have been a good father, at least he did not sexually abuse us the way his mother sexually abused him. At least he broke that cycle. But my father, my father has always been a liar and one thing I know about lying is this: there is nothing people lie about more than the things that they are incapable of admitting to themselves about themselves.

Or maybe he is playing games with truth. Maybe he never sexually abused us. Maybe it was only me. Or maybe he did not sexually abuse us in the ways his mother sexually abused him—each instance of abuse, after all, is unique, and the ways a sober father sexually abuses his son are different than the ways a drunken mother sexually abuses her son. Maybe, in this way, he spoke the truth while lying.

Regardless, a lie told often enough soon becomes a truth. To the teller first of all (because it is the teller who is most desperately in need of believing it) and so, perhaps, after all these years, my father believes himself. I know that we believed him for a very long time.

I don't believe him anymore.

2

It was the fall of 2015. My kids' mom had agreed to settle our custody case and I knew with certainty that no one was going to be able to separate me from my children. I was in an intimate loving and honest relationship, I was two years sober from beer and cigarettes, and I remember thinking, "I've done it." I remember feeling as though I had shed my skin—an old dead skin that had encased me, suffocated me, paralyzed me, nearly killed me—and I was now free to move, to live, to breathe, to be. To be a kind-hearted dad, a loving partner, a devoted brother and uncle, a reliable friend. Anything seemed possible. The several challenges I had faced simultaneously had all, in one way or another, been overcome. I was incredulous and elated. I wept tears of joy and whispered thank you to the trees by the river whom I would secretly hug on my way to work in the morning. I whispered thank you to my children when I rubbed their backs as they fell asleep. I whispered thank you to the gal who loved me as I kissed the nape of her neck and pulled her closer to me.

It was the fall of 2015. I was attending a conference where a speaker was relating sustained illicit drug use to childhood trauma when it happened. I had a memory that didn't quite feel like a memory, a thought that didn't quite feel like a thought, a sensation of having a very small (child-sized) mouth with a penis in it, while also having a memory that didn't quite feel like a memory, a thought that didn't quite feel like a thought, a sensation of having a very large mouth around my very small (child-sized) penis. The only way I have been able to describe this memory that was not a memory, this thought that was not a thought, this sensation, was to say that it felt as though a shard of glass had suddenly been thrust into my brain. Or that it had suddenly emerged from my brain, as if it had been hidden there for years and was only now appearing.

The First Part: Son

I remember being appalled that I was capable of thinking a thought (that was not quite a thought) like this: "How is it possible for such a thing to come into my brain?" I asked myself. "What's wrong with me?"

I am familiar enough with trauma studies to know that the brain, especially the developing brain, does not store and re-member traumas in the same way that it stores and re-members other experiences.[1] But I was still taken aback. Because I am also familiar enough with trauma, including trauma that took place while my brain was developing, to know that I had never experienced a sensation quite like that before. It was incredibly disturbing.

This was the first time I seriously asked myself, "Was I sexually abused as a child?" I was, at that time, thirty-five years old.

---

1. For some of the literature on this see, for example: Levin, *Trauma and Memory*; Maté, *When the Body Says No*; and Van Der Kolk, *The Body Keeps the Score*.

3

I AM NOT INTERESTED in contextualizing my father here. Our culture does enough to contextualize, talk about, sympathize with, and focus upon men like him. Here, now, at this point, it is enough to say that when I was a little boy and I thought I had a fever, he checked my temperature by pulling down my pants and sticking his finger up my ass. He said rectal readings for a fever were more accurate than putting a thermometer in your armpit, or even under your tongue (although that was how he had always checked my temperature before). He didn't tell me what he was going to do before he did it. He just stuck his finger in my ass after pulling down my pants and then told me the rationale afterwards. I remember I was shocked and uncomfortable and frozen. I was surprised that he could tell, with his finger, what my temperature was. I thought maybe it was something he learned in dental school. Because he also used to give us stitches—when I split my knee open, when my brother split the back of my other brother's head open, he was the one who stitched us up—so who knows what all he learned in dental school? Maybe he could also read my temperature by sticking his finger in my ass.

4

These are seven others times when I have frozen.

(1) When a man stopped and asked me for directions at an isolated bus stop in Mississauga and then began to rub the back of his hand on my groin while I was explaining which way to go. This occurred approximately seventeen years ago.

(2) When a female coworker, who was close friends with my supervisor at a residential program for youth experiencing homelessness in Vancouver, a female coworker who was "a touchy feely kind of person" and who practiced Reiki, began to put her hand on my ass instead of my back when she talked to me. I froze no matter where she touched me. She also touched many of the youth in sexual ways. She was only fired (with a nondisclosure agreement, severance package, and generic reference letter) after I filed a complaint and stated I would go public with what had happened to me if appropriate disciplinary action was not taken. This occurred approximately ten years ago.

(3) When I was raped by my friend on his fortieth birthday. This occurred eight years ago.

(4, 5, 6 . . .) When I returned to my ▮▮▮ in ▮▮▮, Ontario, after taking a stress leave due to intervening in a nearly fatal knife fight and ▮▮▮ welcomed me back with ▮▮▮ and then, in the privacy of her office with the door closed, ▮▮▮▮▮▮▮▮▮▮▮▮▮▮▮▮▮▮▮▮▮▮▮. Then, on another day, when she ▮▮▮▮▮▮▮▮ in the lunch room. Then, on another day, when she ▮▮▮▮▮▮▮▮▮▮ when standing beside me in an office doorway. I know that this is sexual harassment (and sexual assault) but I also know how the complaint process favors ▮▮▮ (at this stage, she would be required to undergo sensitivity training but would continue to be ▮▮▮), and I also know that ▮▮▮ is mentally

A Magnificent Work

unwell and can viciously bully people who offend her and so I choose to not report the abuse and simply try to find ways to avoid her.[1]

(7) When returning from a staff day and nearly having a head on collision on the highway due to a driver swerving into our lane and I'm in the back seat on the right and a female coworker, who also is mentally unwell and who also does not respect the physical boundaries of other people, is in the back seat on the left, and she uses the opportunity of the near miss to grab me, as if she is afraid, but she grabs me very high up on my inner thigh and then her hand lingers there. This occurred while I was writing this manuscript.

Freezing has often been my fear reaction. I thought this was due to the physical violence and the constant threat of violence that was a part of life with my father when I was a child. I was always afraid and I was afraid of everything. I spent many years teaching myself not to be afraid or, if I was still afraid, to not permit my fear to determine what I did or didn't do. I believe I have been very successful at this. Consequently, it is interesting to observe that I still have this reaction in a way that feels overpowering, and in a way that still determines my course of action, in situations involving unwanted sexualized physical touch. I still freeze. And the words "no" and "don't touch me" and "get away from me" and "I don't want this" and "what the fuck are you doing?" and a push or a flight or a distancing of myself from that other person—from the sexual assailant, because that's what all of these people are in the situations I describe—don't come. I've always told myself I struggled with this because I'm shy and sensitive and still something of a people pleaser, and, besides, I never want to contribute to other people feeling bad or awkward or mistaken or down on themselves. But this kind of feeling like one cannot say no and, even if one does not want to participate, of feeling like one cannot resist, is common among people who have experienced childhood sexual abuse.

In a complimentary manner, another common experience among some people who have experienced childhood sexual abuse is difficulty initiating sex or sexual contact. I didn't start really learning to do this until I was thirty-four. Until then, with the exception of my wife, I had always dated or had sex with women who took the initiative. I very much wanted to know that the people who were having sex with me, wanted to have sex

---

1. Certain sections of this paragraph have been blacked-out due to an agreement I made when this matter was settled in a pre-trial mediation when I subsequently brought this matter to the Ontario Human Rights Tribunal.

The First Part: Son

with me; I never wanted to force myself onto anyone, and once others initiated, I believe I was a good partner but, still, puzzle pieces are continuing to connect and a certain narrative is becoming increasingly plausible.

5

AND SO I BEGAN to question my sexuality. Are there things about how I approach sex that might suggest that I was sexually abused as a child? I came up with the following list.

Ever since I was very young, I was always able to turn most anything into some kind of sexual joke or innuendo—my friends in high school said there was nothing that I couldn't turn into a penis joke.

I also discovered early on that if I was just the right amount of flirty, an innocent kind of flirty, a flirty that flirts without easily being labeled as flirty, with my friends' moms, then they would do special things for me like send me food when I was living in dorm or pay for me to join their sons on trips.

I flirted with everyone, even if I was not attracted to them—if they found me desirable, I could usually tell very quickly and I fed into that, even if I found nothing about them desirable, and so I flirted with men, with old women, with women I did not find attractive, anyone.

Despite being flirty, I had no sexual contact with anyone, even though opportunities for that contact arose, until I was twenty-one.

Masturbating became my primary self-soothing activity and a secret multi-year porn habit developed and persisted even though I found that I did not like the impact porn seemed to have on my mood or outlook over the longer term and even though I strongly disagreed with much of what constitutes porn.

In my intimate relationships, sex has mattered a great deal to me and, on two occasions, significantly more than it meant to my partner, leading to some issues and complications in those relationships.

I also learned that I enjoyed higher risk sexual activities, sex where there was the risk of being caught, sex in places where sex should not take place; the element of risk and of "doing something I was not supposed to be doing" turned me on a great deal.

I've also always been something of an exhibitionist, doing penis puppetry shows, streaking, and generally looking for opportunities to be naked in public in humorous ways.

All of these things could be taken individually and cumulatively as potential flags related to childhood sexual abuse. But I also wondered: am I pathologizing sexual behaviors that could also just as easily be explained by other things—I made sexual innuendos because I have always been good with words and I learned that jokes like that were the most popular with my peers; I had been kicked out by my own parents as a teenager and so I learned flirting as a survival skill; I was lonely and insecure and so I liked any kind of attention that made me feel special; I had no sexual contact because I was very shy and awkward with girls and then women due to my isolated upbringing; most young men masturbate quite a lot and most also use porn; generally, men are overly focused on sex; having a particular kink doesn't mean abuse took place; and, yes, sometimes nakedness is really just funny.

Maybe looking at things this way is imposing too narrow of a lens onto my sexuality. Maybe looking for clues along these lines becomes a way of writing any kind of story at all. Am I looking for signs of sexual abuse? I will probably find them. Am I looking for signs that I was not sexually abused? I will probably find them.

6

EVER SINCE I WAS very little, I have had nightmares involving giant spiders. The very first one I remember, which I believe was the very first one of them all, occurred when I was about five years old. In my dream I am laying in my bunkbed. I am on my back with my arms by my side, in the middle of my mattress. Suddenly, I see two very large, hairy spider legs come up from over the bottom part of my bed. They place themselves silently on the sides of the bed and more legs follow just as quietly. Then, a large dark hairy spider pulls itself up from below and looms above me as I lie frozen in terror beneath it. I don't remember waking up but every detail of the dream remained with me. When I reflected back on it, I recalled that my father was reading *The Hobbit* to us around this time (I was in kindergarten or Grade 1) and I remember when he read the section about Mirkwood and the spiders there, and I remember him moving his hand on the back of the couch like a spider, and I remember it scared me, and I thought I must have developed a fear of spiders after that. After this first dream, I dreamed a dream about giant spiders approximately once a year for the next thirty years.

(It was also at this time that I developed a reoccurring nightmare about a disembodied hand chasing me through underground tunnels that were a part of an old tomb, although these dreams passed after a few years.)

And then, after I attended the conference about sustained illicit drug use and childhood trauma, and began seriously asking myself the question, "Was I sexually abused as a child?" I had the following dream. It was identical to my very first giant spider dream, and I was, once again, five years old and laying in my bunkbed on my back with my arms by my side, in the middle of my mattress, only this time it was not the large hairy legs of a spider that appeared from the foot of my bed but the large hairy arms of my father and it was his face that appeared and his body that was pulled up over me. "NO," I said in a panic. "I don't want to know this, see this, feel this, remember this. I can't handle any more than this." I was too grossed out by the possibility of actually remembering my dad's mouth on my penis or my dad's penis in my mouth or ass or hands or anywhere on my body—and where would he ejaculate?—and I was equally grossed out and terrified that I might remember what my dad's face looked like when he was sexually aroused and I might know what it was to be the object he was gazing upon while looking that way—and what does his face look like when he cums?—and so I woke up.

I am no longer afraid of spiders and, since then, I have had no giant spider dreams.

7

AFTER MY DREAM, I asked my mother if she had any memory at all or any suspicion at all, of my father sexually abusing me as a child. She was adamant that this could not have happened. She said she made sure to never leave us alone with him long enough for it to happen. This is such an obviously false statement (I remember being alone with him many times—and how much time does a grown man need to pull down a child's pants and stick his finger in that child's ass?) that I immediately regretted asking her.

Having worked with many survivors of all kinds of sexual abuse, I am very familiar with all the ways in which family members often make things worse instead of better. I just didn't expect that to be a factor for me. In retrospect, I imagine everyone who shares things with family members only to be blamed or treated like a liar or dismissed probably didn't think the conversation would go that way. Otherwise, they wouldn't so consistently speak, not only of hurt feelings and disappointment, but of betrayal.

8

THESE ARE SONGS I remember singing in Sunday school when I was very young:

> Trust and obey
> Because there's no other way
> To be happy in Jesus
> But to trust and obey

And also:

> Can a little child like me, Thank the Father fittingly?
> Yes, oh yes! Be good and true, Patient, kind in all you do:
> Love the Lord, and do your part; Learn to say with all your heart:
> Father, we thank thee! Father, we thank thee!

9

My father always made me pull down my pants and underwear before he spanked me.

My mother only made me do this when she wanted the spanking to hurt more. On those occasions, she also tended to use the hairbrush with the firm and pointy bristles. Even then, however, she often left my underwear on.

10

For a time, when my marriage was falling apart, I began to experience uncontrollable priapisms during the night. I would awaken because my penis would be sore from being erect for so long and, unless I got up and walked around for quite some time, putting ice or cold water on it, the erection would not go away. It regularly returned as soon as I fell back asleep again. Even when I did things that would usually make my erection go away—masturbating, having an orgasm during sex—my erection not only did not go away but often hardened (the way your penis feels like it hardens during the moment of climax—that feeling would take place and then not relent).

    I didn't know what to make of this. I went to several medical experts, including a world renowned urologist who worked at the University of British Columbia, and everyone, although they expressed concern (since uncontrollable priapisms can give way to impotence—which is why the blood in any erection sustained for over four hours needs to be drained at the hospital with a rather large needle and, thank god, I always managed to bring it down before it came to that) pronounced me completely healthy. All of them joked, at some point, that people usually came to see them for the opposite reason, "I know a lot of guys who would kill to have your problem." Ha ha ha. That's great. One of them, the kind who wears a brightly colored silly tie in order to remember his humanity, told me he liked my hair when he was knuckles deep in my ass checking my prostate (my prostate was fine, it was always fine, but every doctor insisted on double checking just to be sure the last guy didn't miss anything).

    The doctors were baffled and so was I. I thought maybe it had something to do with all the alcohol I was drinking at the time, although I knew that explanation made no real sense since alcohol generally has the opposite effect on penises. It was only much later that I concluded that the uncontrollable erections were a very odd reaction my body was having to severe stress, just like the muscle cramps I started getting in my chin and around my mouth at that time. These cramps have persisted although the priapisms, for the most part, have not. I can sometimes go weeks feeling my face so cramped up around my mouth (because apparently I am pressing my lips together harder than usual without noticing it, both when I am sleeping and when I am awake) that it becomes difficult to smile or emote in a way that feels natural. This, too, is a very unusual symptom that no doctor has been able to explain or treat. A trauma expert suggested to me that this is the result of me carrying around unresolved childhood traumas or stresses in my body (the body remembers and expresses what the mind forgets or refuses to acknowledge). So, I stood back from the picture and I saw things in a different light.

Why does my body associate pressing my mouth shut tight and unwanted erections with times of severe stress? It seems like there might be a pretty obvious answer to that.

11

I TWICE REMEMBER MY father trying to comfort me when I was sick or sad as a child. The first memory is from the first time I was home schooled—this would have been Grade 2 or 3—and I was sick in bed. It was a Wednesday. I know it was a Wednesday because that was the day my father saw dental patients in the private practice he had built in the lower level of our family home. I remember hearing that my father was going to come up and check on me between patients. And he did come. I remember hearing his footsteps on the stairs and approaching the room along the upstairs hallway. He came into my room wearing his white medical coat. Walking to the side of my bed he placed his hand on my forehead and said a few sympathetic words. Then he left the room and went back downstairs. The whole time, I was completely petrified with fear and doing everything I could not to cry. Previously, when I would remember this event, I thought that I was afraid because I was worried that he would think I was faking sick and that this would result in him hurting me and so, when he said sympathetic words and I nearly cried, because, I thought, I was so surprised and overwhelmed by such a small act of unhoped for yet desperately hoped for kindness, I fought back the tears just in case he saw that as unmanly and decided to hurt me. Now, however, I wonder why I was so afraid of my father's comfort.

The second time was after he had killed my pet rabbit (he said it was an accident and that the rabbit died of fright while my father was trying to give it some medication but, yes, my father has always been a liar). I remember bawling inconsolably and my father actually took me onto his lap to offer me comfort. I remember experiencing no comfort, I remember sitting stiff as a board on his knee, I remember not feeling safe, I remember not wanting to touch him, I remember thinking that I would never be comforted.

12

OTHER CHURCH SONG LYRICS I remember from my childhood include the following:

>This is my father's world
>Oh let me ne'er forget
>That though the wrong
>Seems oft so strong
>He is the ruler yet

13

When I was young, I would sleep on my back in the very middle of my mattress with my arms straight down on either side of me, my legs pressed together, the blanket pulled up to my eyes and, in my imagination, "shaped like a robber's mask." I would lay absolutely still, something that became increasingly painful over time as my limbs fell asleep or itches went unscratched, or as I began to overheat and sweat, but I trained myself to stay that way for long stretches of time (sometimes successfully falling asleep without moving, other times finally rolling over or moving the sheet before falling asleep). I have always remembered this time and, some time a long time ago, I told myself I slept this way because I was afraid of robbers. If robbers break in, they will think I am one of them. If they kill my family, they will bring me with them and I will join their robber clan or group or fictive kinship unit and then, when I am an adult, I will get my revenge on them.

Looking back on it now, I'm not so sure. Spiders that aren't spiders in my dreams, cramps in my face from pressing my mouth shut and priapisms with no medical explanation—perhaps I had other reasons for lying so still, hoping to be overlooked, in a position where both my ass and mouth were hidden.

I don't know.

I do know that I remained afraid of the dark for longer than my little brother. For many years longer. We had a system in place, when we were both afraid of the dark, that if one of us woke up in the night and needed to use the bathroom, then it was permissible to wake up the other one of us and go down the hall to the bathroom together. Eventually, my little brother stopped doing this and started just going to the bathroom on his own. It became increasingly difficult to be the one waking him up, as I was supposed to be older and braver and what did it say about me that my little brother was not afraid of the dark anymore but I still was? I found increasingly implausible reasons to wake him—pretending to wake up after I woke him up, pretending that I thought he had asked me to go to the bathroom with him, but eventually I stopped asking and forced myself to hold it or, if I absolutely could not, I climbed in a frenzied panic out of my bunkbed (step one), stumbled to the door of my room (step two), looked down the hallway and at the other bedroom doorways (step three—and to also see if the bathroom was already occupied), and then rushed into the bathroom as swiftly and quietly as possible, turning on the light and closing and locking the door in a single motion (step four). On the way back, I always debated with myself as to whether I should first look out the door before turning off the bathroom light (and risk waking my parents? And risk seeing some monstrous thing in the dark I did not want to see?) or if I simply wanted to go blindly and as swiftly as possible from the bathroom back into my bed.

14

Why, out of four sons, was I the one who was kicked out? Was I really that much worse than all of my brothers? Or was my father trying to rid himself of that which could destroy him? Destroy my credibility, destroy my character, destroy my future, destroy me, and who else can stand up at his funeral and say, "My father, in his own defense, often said that although he may not have been a good father, at least he did not sexually abuse us the way his mother sexually abused him. At least he broke that cycle. But my father, my father has always been a liar..."

15

As I was trying to make sense of the shard of glass in my brain, another memory came to mind. It was 2005 and I was working night shifts at a residential program for youth experiencing homelessness. The current group of residents was on a horror movie kick and decided to watch James Wan's film, *Saw* (2004). I wasn't much for torture porn but tried to sit it out with them in order to work on building some relationships and to see where it might lead us in conversation. It was a grotesquely violent film with some horrendous scenes but, to my surprise, these were not the ones that stayed with me. Because one scene did stay with me. It was this one:

A small girl is convinced that there is an intruder in her room and, although her dad comes and looks under the bed and comforts her and treats it like the case of a kid imagining monsters, before the scene concludes the camera zooms in on the closet at the foot of the girl's bed and we discover that a strange man is lurking there.

Out of everything in that movie, this scene scared me so badly that I actually slept with the lights on for the next few nights. I was twenty-five years old. There was a closet at the foot of my bed in the room I was renting in a house full of graduate students and I was, seemingly inexplicably, terrified that there was a strange man in it who wanted to hurt me.

There was also a closet at the foot of my bed when I was a child. It was very large, about two feet deep and covering one whole side of the room. When I was very little it had mirrors on it and then these were converted into blackboards when my little brother and I were homeschooled. Sometime around the time I was six, my little brother who would have been four or five then, was playing in that closet with the adopted daughter of my parents' blind friends and they were whispering and giggling and my father came in and dragged my brother out and gave him a beating somewhere out of sight from the rest of us. I don't know what he thought was going on

The First Part: Son

in the closet. I wonder now if he was worried that his actions therein might be repeated by his children.

(Was my brother also abused? Or, since we shared a room, did he witness me being abused? He would have only been a few years old at the time.)

I dreamed about this closet last week. I was back in my childhood home (earlier that week, my father had offered to sell it to me so I could "hold on to all the fond childhood memories" but I bit my tongue and, instead of burning the house down with him inside, I said no thanks), and there were new people living there. I was in my old bedroom and wasps kept getting in and almost getting tangled up in my hair and in the hair of the new children living there. I was concerned that they might get stung and so I checked the window screen but everything was in order. Eventually, I realized that the wasps were coming from the closet and that there was probably a nest in there. So, I layered on long clothing, put on a snow suit, goggles, a mask and hood, and prepared to open the closet. And then I woke up.

I took this as a sign of progress.

I think my mind was trying to make progress on some of these things when I was younger, but I wasn't prepared for it. When I was twenty-three, two years before I had my experience with the *Saw* movie, I was living in a basement apartment on Dundas St. in Toronto and I had a series of nightmares that scared me more than any other dreams I have had. In these nightmares, an evil presence, intent on doing me harm, was looming over my bed watching me while I slept. I would awake in a panic but, unlike other nightmares, the feeling of being watched by a malevolent presence would not fade and I would often lay awake for a considerable amount of time, too terrified to move. Finally, after a week, I dreamed this dream again and forced myself to get up and go to the bathroom. I turned on the light and splashed some water on my face to try and calm myself, but when I straightened up and looked at my reflection in the mirror, I saw a man standing behind me. He had long hair hanging over his face and long dirty fingers which were reaching around my neck. And then I woke up. This was the only time I have ever had a dream within a dream (until then, I did not know such things were possible outside of horror movies).

The catch is that the man in the mirror looked like my dad when he was a young man and had long hair and a goatee. I have no memories of seeing my dad that way. I only know he once looked like that because of pictures I have seen.

A Magnificent Work

At that time, I made no connections between those dreams and the possibility of having experienced childhood sexual abuse. I was solely concerned with having the dreams stop—I was scared to go to bed for many nights—but, after the dream within a dream, they did.

I only really made the connection between these dreams, the *Saw* experience, and the closet in my bedroom when I was a child, after a friend told me she was worried about me because she had a dream about me and realized that my kindness and my commitment to gentleness, were covering a very great darkness that was at my core. In the middle of this darkness she said there was an old crone, a very wicked presence, who was blocking me from knowing some things or developing in certain ways. I asked her what this crone looked like and she said "an old perversely twisted image of you." I was taken aback by this and then suddenly thought to show her a picture of my father. "Yes," she said visibly repulsed, "that's who I saw," and she could barely stand to look at him.

That's when I decided to start this manuscript. Because, after two years of asking myself if I was sexually abused as a child, I had not made any progress.

16

WHEN A FRIEND MENTIONED to her therapist mother that I used to bounce my head off of my pillow in order to fall asleep at night, and also on the couch during the day, her mother's face expressed concern (she looked disturbed). She said that this symptom tended to only manifest in children who are on the autism spectrum or who have suffered some combination of emotional abuse and neglect.

I wouldn't be surprised if I registered as having some kind of high functioning Asperger's, and I've certainly suffered physical and emotional abuse and neglect as a child. These things alone are enough to make my dad the subject of my nightmares. I had many very good reasons to fear him as a child. I'm not eager to also believe that he sexually abused me. In fact, many professionals suggest that trying to recover memories that are lost is not necessarily a good thing and may, counterproductively, produce false memories (although all memories are reconstructive processes and so everything is on a continuum of accuracy). Instead, these professionals suggest that one should ask why one wants to know if one was sexually abused as a child—and what difference that knowledge might make. (And, if one concludes that one was sexually abused as a child, the focus falls, not on the abuse itself, but on understanding the strengths and other coping mechanisms one developed to get through the abuse.)

17

I have two older brothers. Shortly after their thirteenth birthdays, they were taken downstairs and given "the sex talk" by my father. When I came to my thirteenth birthday, my father never gave me the talk. I was very interested in it. I wanted to know about sex. It was a mystery I was keen to learn more about. I believe I had already found the Sear's catalogue on my parents' bookcase. The bra section excited me most although, once I noticed those pages getting dog-eared (whereas other sections were not) I became concerned and then, to my dismay, it disappeared altogether one day. Thankfully, in the Wishbook that came in the mail every Christmas, there was also a special lingerie section. I believe my feelings around sex were not unusual and were similar to what other boys of that age experience.

However, my father did not have the sex talk with me. I waited and waited but he never brought it up. And so, building up my courage, I eventually reminded him that he had promised to have the sex talk with me (reminding my father of any of the promises he didn't keep was always a high-risk activity but, in this case, my curiosity won out). Then my father laughed at me. He pointed at me in front of my brothers and suggested I must be a particularly horny young man to be so eager to know these things. I remember my brothers laughed, too. And still he didn't give me the sex talk. I reminded him again. "Yes, yes," he said, "we'll get to that—but not now." And so I waited and reminded him a third time. Then, instead of giving me the sex talk, he took me downstairs, gave me a few books about sex and told me to read them. He went back upstairs and I read the books, paying special attention to the pictures. He came down again a little later on and asked me if I understood. I said I did.

He gave the sex talk to my younger brother the following year shortly after his thirteenth birthday.

The First Part: Son

The question, then, is this: was there a reason why my father gave the sex talk to all of my brothers but did not give it to me? Was he afraid that I would ask, "Oh, so what you did to me when I was young—was that sex?" Is that why he mocked me in front of my brothers when I raised the subject? Because he wanted others to believe that there was something wrong with me when it came to sex and that way, if I ever accused him of anything, he would already have paved the way for me not to be taken seriously?

When I was a child, I searched and I searched, trying to understand what prompted my father to be violent or cruel because, I thought, if I understood, I would be able to avoid being hurt. I never was able to understand and came to believe that his violence was nonsensical. It operated without rhyme or reason. It had no causes outside of himself. Certain things, however, make more sense now.

Like why my father was constantly spending time alone in the basement, painting miniature figures for war games or playing on his computer. Even during family gatherings, when my grandparents visited or during family game times with just my parents and brothers, the question was always—would my father come up to join us? And, if he did, what kind of mood would he be in? Looking back now my question is this: did he isolate himself in the basement because he was battling the desire to touch or fuck or be sucked off by his children? Was I the one where the urges won out over the desire to resist?

18

AND THIS ONE, TOO:

>Coming in the name of Jesus,
>Grace we seek with one accord
>Not to do the things that please us,
>But the things that please our Lord.
>Foll'wing him with our endeavor,
>To our promise keeping true;
>Striving still to do whatever
>He would like to have us do.

19

SOMETIMES, I FEEL COMPELLED to write. I don't know where this compulsion comes from, but it has come and gone for as long as I can remember. When it is very strong, I often do the kind of writing I like the most. When it wanes, I don't write. Outside of an academic context, I am an undisciplined writer. I don't write "x" number of words every day or do the different exercises they suggest for people who want to be writers. I write when I want to, when I can.

I gave myself a break from processing some of these things because I felt that I had come to a dead-end. No other memories were coming back to me, no more puzzle pieces were falling together, no more shards of glass were appearing from nowhere in my brain, and so, although frustrated, I stopped exploring the subject. At the suggestion of trauma expert, I did some somatic experiencing therapy and I found that useful for being more connected with my body and better coping with stress, but I don't know that it got me anywhere in relation to questions I had about childhood sexual abuse.

During my break, I was reading a lot of W. G. Sebald's melancholic travelogues and thinking about how they compare to Cormac McCarthy's presentation of violence as a part of the very essence of all that is.[1] When McCarthy writes, it feels as though he wants to kick the reader in the chest. Reading is books is an almost traumatic experience. Their words take the wind out of you, knock you over, break your heart, make you love and weep. Their words are like a revelation, an apocalypse. Sebald is very different. He does not seek to formulate the perfect revelatory combination of words but, I think, operates from the premise that some things are, quite literally, unspeakable (and Sebald is no less apocalyptic for writing in this

---

[1]. For readers interested in exploring these writers, I especially recommend the following: Sebald, *Austerlitz*; Sebald, *The Rings of Saturn*; Sebald, *The Emigrants*; McCarthy, *Blood Meridian*; and McCarthy, *The Border Trilogy*.

A Magnificent Work

way). Therefore, instead of hitting you as hard as he possibly can with what he is trying to understand or reveal, you find Sebald circling around a very big darkness. There is a void in the center of his work but the void is not formless and there are unspeakable things moving in it. We begin to get a sense for them, and for their massive scale, as we spiral around the void, moving closer, dancing away, the whole thing too immense and too veiled to be taken in all at once but, here, one catches a glimpse, and, there, there is an opening. As this dance is maintained over the course of a novel, something substantial is built. Something that feels more monumental, more ontological, than the fiery flashes of feeling prompted by McCarthy. McCarthy knocked me down, but I got back up again. Sebald didn't touch me, but I've been limping ever since I started reading him.

As I was considering these things I wondered if I could write in the manner of Sebald. Could I also write in a way that circled around something so terribly big and unspeakable, without actually mentioning that something, and yet, partially for that reason, be able to better communicate that something? Without knowing where I was going to go, the first sentence of the following short story appeared fully formed in my head and the rest followed immediately after.

> It was the Whining of the Dog
>
> It was the whining of the dog that he heard. The dog whining, just outside the door. He could, and he did, picture it with its muzzle between its front paws, thrust down into the floor, and its eyebrows raised in that way dogs raise their eyebrows when they have their chins down but they are looking up at you. Its tail was wagging in that way dogs wag their tails when they are sorry even though they can't figure out what they did wrong. Whining, and the thump, thump, thump, of the tail as it hit the wall that separated the bedroom from the upper hallway. It wasn't the hands on his body (although hands on bodies are not soundless). It wasn't the fingers in his mouth (although fingers in mouths make noise). It was the whining of the dog.
>
> He wanted to comfort the dog and explain to it that it wasn't the dog's fault and he wanted to give it a treat and he wanted to take it with him when he left but he didn't know leaving and he didn't know speaking and "It's okay, it's okay, it's okay," he thought over and over and over and over and over and over and over and over and thump, thump, thump, thump, thump, thump, thump, thump, thump, and the whining of the dog. And, "I'm sorry, too," he thought, and he raised his eyebrows and tried to look up but he couldn't.

The First Part: Son

I was content with my efforts. Four months later I realized that I was describing my childhood bedroom (I can see the wall that separated the bedroom from the upper hallway) and I remembered the white German Shepherd we had when I was very little. I reconsidered how this story came into my head fully formed. Was this another shard of glass? A memory not quite a memory, a thought not quite a thought? What exactly is the void I am circling around here?

20

I DO REMEMBER SEEING my father naked when I was very young. He was walking from his bedroom, down the upstairs hallway, to the bathroom. I remember he was hairy and his penis looked impossibly big, thick and veiny, with a swollen head. I remember he would also sometimes sit naked on the toilet and leave the door open. I remember this feeling gross.

21

BEFORE I DREAMED THAT my father was the spider but after the shard of glass appeared in my brain, I dreamed this dream.

I am back at the house where I grew up. Things happen that I don't remember. This takes up most of the dream. And then I remember the ending. I am sitting and writing (by hand with a loose pile of printer paper) at a rough wooden table in front of the shed in the backyard, facing out the gate down the driveway. I notice a large brown spider on the corner of the house. Ugh, that's a horrid looking spider, I think. Just as I think that, a similar spider lowers itself from the roof of the shed into my hair. I immediately go to brush it out of my hair with my hand and another very large spider lands on the back of my hand. I panic and get up to brush myself off. I jump and yell "fuck!" over and over . . . and then I notice that there are other spiders hanging from the house and shed and trees and lattice and I have to dodge them as I jump around. I turn around to walk back to my writing, or possibly leave out the back gate, but the wind picks up and blows a wall of hanging spiders into the front of me, covering me from head to toe (although I do get my arms up in time, like a boxer, to protect my face). I fall over more from the horror than from anything else. I then wake up. Both my hands are asleep from my third finger to my pinky finger. It has been a long time since that has happened. Not since my year of heavy drinking have my hands gone numb in my sleep.

This dream is similar to another spider dream I had when I tried to explore an abandoned farmhouse but could not get in the door because the darkness inside was impenetrable. I walked away from the house through an orchard of trees covered in strange purple fruits. Picking one of the fruits, I realized it was a spider hanging from the tree, all the fruits were spiders, and, once I realized this, they all began to drop from the trees and run at me, up me, over me, as I ran in terror through the orchard. I forced

A Magnificent Work

a stream to appear in my dream and I dove into it but the spiders cast their webs across the water and ran across, dropping onto my head as I swam and clinging to my hair when I dove, more falling onto me every time I came up for air.

These dreams are similar to the dreams my mother has for eight months in a row, ten years after leaving my father, when she began to dream that she is back at the house where I grew up and she is in the basement and it is full of giant spiders who, in turn, are covered in millions of tiny spiders and, the more she swats them, the more they multiply.

22

My mother lets go of my hand and leaves the room. It is a very large room. It is full of very noisy children. I, too, am a child. It is the Sunday school class for the youngest children. That means I am probably five years old. There are toys I want to play with, a lot of toys, toys I never get to have at home, and I want to play with them but there is a crowd of kids and they are noisy and most of them are bigger than me and I don't know any of them and they are running around and I don't know anyone and I'm scared and I can't move and I stand with my arms by my side and I begin to cry. One of the girls supervising the Sunday school class (she is how old—twelve? Thirteen?) tries to console me but I am not consolable. I continue to cry. Only I cry harder because I want to be comforted, I want her words to be true, I want it all to be okay, but it's not, it can't be, it never will be. And I am ashamed that I am crying, here, in front of all the other kids standing frozen by the door with my arms by my side. The girl hugs me but I can't move. I cry because I want my mother but I know that if they have to send for my parents I will be in trouble. But I want my mother to come and comfort me. I cannot stop crying. And so they send a messenger to notify my parents. The messenger will have to walk into the sanctuary and interrupt my parents in the act of singing or, even worse, in the quiet when everyone is listening to the sermon, one of my parents will have to get up and, while everyone watches, walk out to deal with a kid that is obviously out of control. My dad will feel angry and humiliated. I hope my mom comes.

I'm standing by the door and the other kids are sitting in a large circle and singing:

> Jesus loves me this I know
> For the Bible tells me so
> Little ones to him belong
> They are weak but he is strong

A Magnificent Work

Yes, Jesus loves me
Yes, Jesus loves me
Yes, Jesus loves me
The Bible tells me so

My father arrives at the door. (*My memory fractures*) I know he is angry but he is trying to hide it. I see it though. I feel it. He takes my hand and now I am unfrozen. I walk out of class with him. (*Jesus loves me this I know*) He takes me into the stairwell of the church. Nobody else is there. He hits me, knocks me into the wall. This is not the first time. I am crumpled in a ball on the floor still crying. (*For the Bible tells me so*) He tells me how disgusted he is by my weakness, by my inability to be a proper boy, and he intends to give me something to cry about every time I cry for no reason. He doesn't use words like these, at least I don't think so, I don't remember his exact words (apart from the "something to cry about" line he often used), but I see the scene. Him looming over me. The empty stairwell in the church. Me curled up in the corner against the wall crying. It goes on forever and ever, it never changes, it has no end.

My father arrives at the door. (*My memory fractures*) I know he is angry but he is trying to hide it. I see it though. I feel it. He takes my hand and now I am unfrozen. I walk out of class with him, out of church with him, and into the minivan in the parking lot. (*Little ones to him belong*) He tells me to get into the front of the van with him. I am surprised. I am too small to be allowed in the front of the van. Perhaps he will try to console me. (*They are weak but he is strong*) He tells me to turn around and pulls down my pants. (*Yes*)

    The void is here.

           I remember only pain and wanting it to stop and I remember it lasting as long as he wanted it to last.

    (*Jesus*)

    He tells me to pull up my pants. He gives me toilet paper to clean up my face.

(*loves me*)

He holds my hand and, as we walk back into church, he ensures that I am smiling.

(*Yes*)

23

How often when in sickness, your body racked with pain,
This knocking resounded in your ears;
How often in the nighttime the knock would come again?
So loud it would fill your soul with fears.
Oh, don't you hear him knocking at the door?
He's knocking at the door to come in;
He wants an invitation to cross your threshold o'er,
Then Jesus will save you from all sin.
Why will you keep him knocking? Why won't you let him in?
He'll fill your pathway with delight;
That hand so torn and bleeding will wash away your sin,
Oh, welcome the Savior in tonight.
Oh, don't you hear him knocking at the door?
He's knocking at the door to come in;
He wants an invitation to cross your threshold o'er,
Then Jesus will save you from all sin.

24

Did he hit me in the church stairwell or did he spank me? I also seem to remember being spanked in the church stairwell—I remember feeling shocked that he would pull my pants down there (or did he pull my pants down there?)—and I also remember another time laying crumpled against a wall at home because my dad had hit me in the face, knocked me into the wall, and then proceeded to kick me while I was down. Or did all these things happen at different times? Were there three different stairwell spankings or beatings at the church? I imagine at least that many—I remember my fear of my dad coming to punish me was part of what made it hard for me to stop crying in Sunday School and the whole thing turned into a vicious spiral which, to me as a child, led me to blame myself for the abuse I experienced—but memories of traumas are not like other memories. And all memories, it should be recalled, are creative reconstructions.

25

I HAVE BEEN WORKING through *The Sexual Healing Journey: A Guide for Survivors of Sexual Abuse* (the newly revised and updated third edition) by Wendy Maltz, and one of the strategies she says some people who have experienced childhood sexual abuse find useful is this: imagine your adult self being present with your child self when that child self is feeling hurt, alone, and in need of comfort (a child self, some people suggest, that remains a part of us even after we are done growing up).[1] Imagine soothing this child and imagine being the kind of adult to that child that that child needed in that moment.

Yesterday, when I was writing and rewriting and editing and reading and rereading what I wrote about what I could remember from Sunday School, when I saw myself again on the floor, against the wall, in a stairwell, with my father looming over me, his rage and disgust and hands overwhelming me, I tried this strategy. I imagined my adult self entering into that stairwell and picking that boy up off the floor, cradling him in my arms, kissing his tears from his cheek, and telling him that everything was going to be okay now. When I got to this point in my imagination, I burst into sobs I could not suppress and I could go no further. Because everything was not going to be okay. Because I couldn't take that child away from that place. Because nobody ever did and that child will, forever, be without comfort.

Today I stayed in bed all day.

---

1. See Maltz, *The Sexual Healing Journey*, 126.

26

When I eat bread or buns, I almost always choke. It's like my throat has stopped lubricating itself and the dough sticks right at the top of my trachea and I cough or scramble for water and, over the last ten years, I've become a master of unchoking myself. It became something of a joke between my wife and I. But what causes a condition like this? As far as the doctors can tell, there is no medical explanation for this sudden drying of my throat, this inability to swallow, this constantly choking because, for whatever reason, my body is suddenly saying that it doesn't want anything in the back of my mouth, going down my throat.

27

IN OCTOBER OF 2016, I went to Lawrence Paul Yuxweluptun's "Unceded Territories" show at the Vancouver Museum of Anthropology. His paintings impacted me quite deeply, as did the spirit in which he spoke to us, and the way he shook my hand and looked into my eyes when I said "thank you" to him afterwards because I didn't know what more I could say. "You're welcome," he said and he held my hand and gaze a moment and then I broke away because he was trying to leave and I didn't want to hold him back. And what else could I have said, anyway?

In one of the rooms in the gallery, I come around a corner and, suddenly, at my feet, there is a large white cross on the ground in front of me and when I look at the cross I realize that it is made of many, many pairs of boy's underwear, and when I look closer at the cross I realize that at the back of each pair of underwear is a red drop or two of blood, and then I look at the name of this piece and I see that it is called "Residential School Dirty Laundry" and now I can hardly breath and I kind of gasp, kind of groan, and the air passes out of my body and, for a while (how long is a while?), it doesn't return to me and I almost start sobbing uncontrollably but I stop myself because I'm not sure what to think of white tears in a space like this and so, instead, I sit down because I can't stand up anymore, and I stare at this cross and I stare, and then the air comes back into my body and I breathe again and I see others in this little space and they mostly glance at the cross for a moment before moving on to the other pieces around it, but I sit and I breathe and I start to feel my body again and eventually I stand up and then, because I can't stay there forever, because I can't lay down and not get back up again, because I have remembered that I am still alive, I walk out of the gallery. (I had to write this paragraph in the second person to relive it and then I went back through it to change everything to the first person.)

A Magnificent Work

~

Shortly after this, I saw Tanya Tagaq (for the second time), at a church in Toronto. Seeing her is like no other experience I have ever had. When she sings, I see things. I wrote a poem to try and describe this. I called it "Tanya Tagaq Revisited (with Lawrence Paul Yuxweluptun)". It's a long poem and not entirely relevant to this but this first part I want to quote goes like this:

> There is a boy and he is six and he is in the washroom and there is blood in the back of his underwear and he is afraid of what the sisters will do if they see that he has ruined the clothes they gave him.
> Where are my children?
> They took his clothes and his hair and his name and there is blood in the back of his underwear and he is afraid of what the sisters will do if they see that he has ruined the clothes they gave him.
> There is a hole in the sky and a boy with blood in his underwear and a voice that asks me, do you want to see all of the boys? I will show them to you. Then they begin to walk in front of me. Boy after boy. All dressed the same. All wearing numbers. All with the same haircut. All alone. All with blood in their underwear. They crowd out my vision. They are very young and very small but still they fill up the inside and outside of everything. There is no more room for them but still they are coming. The edges of space and time begin to tear to make room for them all.
> No! I don't want to see anymore! The vision stops.

The poem then goes on for a while but the boy returns and I change to the first-person voice:

> There is a boy on the beach holding starfish, there is a boat on the horizon that is a hole in the sky. There is a man who has lost his children. There is a mother whose children were taken. There is blood in the soil, the soil is blood, the blood is the soil. And the rectums of children are not tabernacles designed to host the penises of men.
> I used to think that if I was good enough, they would send me home. But they didn't send me home. I thought, perhaps, if I misbehaved enough, they would send me home. But they didn't send me home. I thought if I submitted enough, they would send me home. But they didn't send me home. There is blood in the back of my underwear and I am afraid of what the sisters will do when they see that I have ruined the clothes they gave me.

The First Part: Son

The poem continues on after that. But what strikes me now is how I identified with the six year old boy with blood in the back of his underwear who is afraid that he will get in trouble because he dirtied his clothes (because, in the only world he knows, blood in the back of his underwear will ever only be his fault). Why is this part of what I saw?

28

Deep and wide
Deep and wide
There's a fountain flowing deep and wide
Deep and wide
Deep and wide
There's a fountain flowing deep and wide
Hmmm and wide
Hmmm and wide
There's a fountain flowing hmmm and wide
Hmmm and wide
Hmmm and wide
There's a fountain flowing hmmm and wide
Hmmm and hmmm
Hmmm and hmmm
There's a fountain flowing hmmm and hmmm
Hmmm and hmmm
Hmmm and hmmm
There's a fountain flowing hmmm and hmmm
Hmmm and hmmm
Hmmm and hmmm
Hmmm hmmm hmmm hmmm flowing hmmm and hmmm
Hmmm and hmmm
Hmmm and hmmm
Hmmm hmmm hmmm hmmm flowing hmmm and hmmm
Hmmm hmmm hmmm
Hmmm hmmm hmmm
Hmmm hmmm hmmm hmmm hmmm hmmm hmmm hmmm
Hmmm hmmm hmmm
Hmmm hmmm hmmm
Hmmm hmmm hmmm hmmm hmmm hmmm hmmm hmmm

First Intermission

ONCE WERE CHILDREN: A POEM FOR MY OLDEST BROTHER ON THE OCCASION OF HIS BIRTHDAY

I.

I SAW A PICTURE of you today when you were a child. You had a gentle smile. You look shy and sweet and tender—like the kind of kid who wouldn't say a word if he was abused. And you didn't. None of us did. But for you abuse has just steadily been overshadowed by chronic pain, long-term illness, and dis-ease. Yet, for the most part, you still don't say a word.

(I've been thinking how strange it is that I used to describe our childhood as "sheltered." I think the term "deliberately isolated" might better capture what was going on. It wasn't that our parents were trying to protect us from the evil out there in the world—it's that our dad didn't want others to know the evil we experienced at home.)

II.

I saw a picture of you today when you were a baby. You are peering over the edge of an old-school baby stroller—that kind that you see and think maybe it's actually called a pram. You remind me of my own babies and I think, hey, once upon a time you, too, were brand new. Once upon a time you, too, were thrown into a world not of your choosing. Once upon a time you were innocent and, before you had a chance to be anything else, you were beaten and you were altered so that pain would forever be a part of your life . . . and you've just been finding your way from there. As best you can, however you can, finding your way from there.

A Magnificent Work

We were all of us innocent, once upon a time. We were all of us longing to love and be loved. We were all of us full of wonder—but for you and me and our other brothers, our wonder all too quickly turned to fear. Instead of embracing the world into which we had been thrown we retreated into ourselves—we looked for escape in books or music or computer games or working late shifts just in order to be away from our house. Because the world wasn't full of wonder for us. It was a place that only appeared to be safe but where violence could erupt at any time for no perceptible reason.

III.

I saw a picture of you today when you were a young man. You still looked happy then. Like there was still a joy and sense of adventure inside of you. Perhaps even something to look forward to in life. You are beautiful. Your smile is still gentle and I can connect the shy and sweet and tender boy I remember with this young man in the picture.

Forty isn't old but it isn't young either (they say age is just a number . . . but the "they" who say that are always old). Life has taken you and I places where we never wanted to go. Death has been a constant companion for both of us and some days, when the sorrow and loss and heartbreak and unfulfilled dreams and physical pain become a little more intense than their usual intensities, Death feels more like an old friend than an old enemy. I don't ever remember praying for anyone else to die but, back when I used to pray (the kind of prayers one writes in one's mind like letters to God), I prayed that for you. Mostly though, over the years, I have longed to hold you in my arms and cover your face with kisses and love you so much and so strongly that it takes your pain away. I know your wife feels the same way.

IV.

I saw a picture of you today as a father. Your sons have gentle smiles. They look shy and sweet and tender. They look hilarious and silly and delighted to be with their dad. As for me, what have I learned in life? That being a loving father is the greatest thing I will ever do—and even though we are all smaller than grains of sand on the beach, and even though our lives pass faster than the blink of an eye, and even though millions came before us and millions will come after us and soon we will, all of us, disappear just like when we never were—even in light of all of this, being a loving father is no small thing. I suspect we all mean less than nothing, perhaps some days you agree with me, but I'm not convinced meaning has anything to do with love. Loving is good, even if goodness doesn't exist. And when your children climb up into your lap because they feel sad or sick or hurt themselves playing, and you wrap your arms around them and I see them nuzzle into you that, too, is good. It is very good.

I don't remember our dad showing us that kind of affection. But I do remember, after your first surgery, even saying that phrase "your first surgery" is appalling, but I remember after your first surgery when you were at our parents' house and you were curled up in pain on their bathroom floor and you had vomited and your abdominal incision had ripped open and I could see inside your body and our father came in and looked at you with something I understood to be disgust and our father said "either go back to bed or go back to the hospital but don't just lie there on the bathroom floor" and then our father turned and left the room and didn't say anything else or offer any help as I carried you out to the van and some days when I remember this I still get the urge to go to his house and ring the doorbell and then kick his teeth in.

Yes, being a loving father is no small thing. And it is no small thing that you hold your children in your arms when they aren't feeling well and it is no small thing that they seek out your arms at those times.

V.

I saw a picture of you today when you were married. We all still look like puppies then—youthful faces and flat stomachs and smiles that look like that came more easily. I think both you and your wife were hesitant to get into a relationship at first because you had both been hurt in the past. Being rejected by someone you love, and who you think loves you, is a strange and devastating and alienating experience. In some ways, it is more traumatic than death for, while death is tragic, in part, because you are forever separated from someone you love, in death the separation is (usually) not a choice. Part of what is so hard about rejection is that a person is *choosing* to reject you and *choosing* to live forever separated from you. But as you and your wife fell in love, I think you felt safe loving and being loved by each other. That, too, is no small thing. As you continue to recover from your second surgery, and continue coming to grips with the recognition that the surgery did not heal you as much as we all hoped, I hope you and your wife will continue to communicate to each other that the relationship you have is a safe place to love and be loved. Pain tends to isolate us and you both have experienced a lot of pain in recent years. Isolation, in turn, when experienced by someone in a relationship can be experienced by the other person in that relationship as rejection. I hope you both continue to find ways to say, "I am not rejecting you. I love you. I love being loved by you. We can get through this together."

VI.

Once we were children. Now we are not. Once we were young. Now we are not. But we can still be kind, we can still be gentle, we can still be sweet, and tender, and shy, and hilarious and silly. Only now, in the last few years, have I been recovering the sense of wonder that was stolen from us and replaced with fear when we were kids. I don't know how much pain will permit you to recover that wonder yourself, but I see it coming through sometimes when you are with your family.

    I love you, brother. For you today my heart is full of joy and sorrow, love and longing, and sometimes in dreams that carry us well beyond hope and hopelessness, I walk hand-in-hand with you in a place that feels like peace.

The Second Part

Father

"Daddy, don't see any monsters. But just kill the monsters."[1]

---

1. My daughter, three-and-one-half years old, in a conversation with me.

1

He is running from puddle to puddle and jumping over the cracks in the sidewalk and I am running beside him, catching him by the coat whenever he starts to fall. He is laughing and making that gurgling noise he makes in his throat when he is extra happy. He is four years old. I am thirty-three.

2

A MONTH LATER, I was cuddling him and he rolled over and put his arm around me and put his head on my chest and looked up at me and kissed me on the chin and said, "Daddy, you're my best friend."

3

IN THE WINTER OF 2009, my son was born on the living room couch, his mother naked on all fours, having come out of the pool because the midwives were worried that his heart rate had dropped. After, when she was birthing the placenta, a bubble of blood that had formed on the side of it burst and sent a spray six feet up the living room wall and flooding down behind the couch. "That's the biggest placenta I've seen in twenty years!" the midwife said, as I stared at the splatter pattern. I hadn't thought to put any tarps there. The cat became hysterical, panting and refusing food and, for the next week, I had to inject water into the nape of his neck to prevent him from becoming dehydrated. The water would stay in a ball under his fur and then, slowly, absorb into his body. After a week he stopped panicking. My son took about nine months longer than that.

My daughter was born in the water in a pool I inflated in the kids' room, in the summer of 2011. I remember the way her mother's body bulged outwards as she was crowning, my daughter's hair briefly appearing and then receding, appearing and receding, with each contraction. The midwives encouraged me to stroke the top of her head every time for a moment before it retreated back again into her mother's body. I did not know a body could bulge in that way. I caught her when she came out and carried her into the world of air, of spirit, and of wailing amidst professions of love.

4

HE IS FIVE AND she is three. It is well passed their bedtime. There is garbled yelling from their room.

    Me: Kids, please be quiet!

    Her: I'm being quiet!

    Him: I'm being quiet!

    Me: Okay, thank you!

    Her: I'm being quiet!

    Him: I'm being quiet!

    Both of them together: *I'm being quiet!*

    Me: . . .

    Her: I'm being quiet! I'm being quiet! I'm being quiet!

5

When my wife and I finally separated, my son, who had just turned four at the time, would weep inconsolably before he became accustomed to the joint custody rotation. When his mother dropped him off, he would cry over and over again, "I've lost my mommy! I've lost my mommy! I've lost my mommy! I've lost my mommyI'velost my mommy I'velostmym om mmyI'velostmymommyI'vI'veloI IIII!" And it would be one long heart-rending sob as he climbed onto my bed and then onto the window ledge to see if he could find her outside. There was nothing I could say at those times that would comfort him. He was forlorn, devastated, afraid, and seeking something I could not give him. Eventually, I learned that I had to allow him to cry himself out and leave him some space to mourn, before he could climb back down from the window ledge, emerge from my room, and begin to recognize other things and people.

It is no easy thing for a father to hear his son cry in this way. He cried in this way for the first nine months of his life, although, at that time, he did it wordlessly. Day and night, he cried. He cried and hardly slept. Everything that people suggested for babies with colic didn't work. Eventually, we learned that the only thing that would gradually settle him down was holding him in our arms while bouncing on a Pilates ball. Then, he would sleep. But he would awaken as soon as we stopped bouncing and instantly begin to cry again. I didn't know if we were doing something wrong, I didn't know what else I could do, I didn't know if this meant that I was a bad father or a bad person, and sometimes I became angry at him and just left him in his crib to cry by himself (it didn't make a difference—he just kept crying, often so hard that he would make himself vomit, so I didn't try that approach for very long), and then I did feel like a bad father and I didn't know what to do with these feelings of love and fear and anger and uncertainty and how they all mixed together or what they said about me and how could I be angry at

A Magnificent Work

someone so innocent who was only in pain (or so it seemed) and how could I want to get away from someone I wanted to love or thought I loved but whom I fled for the pub to binge drink on weekends because my marriage, my life, my dreams, and the things I did that I thought gave me meaning, all of these things were in utter ruins.

Shortly after the colic finally passed, my wife booked a one way ticket for him and her to the other side of the country so she could spend some time living with her mom, and this time it was I who cried inconsolably as I held him in my arms in an empty airport late at night outside the security clearance, because I didn't know if or when I was going to see him again, because I didn't know if I was going to live or die and, even if I lived, I didn't know if he would come back or I would go after him, and I held him in my arms and he was sleeping and he was beautiful and he was tiny and he was flawless and then he was gone and I walked back out of the airport weeping, and weeping, and weeping. A few nights later, I was drunk and all the bars were closed and I sat on the railing of a bridge and I put my wallet on the ledge beside me so that it would be easier to identify my body, and as I prepared to fall off the face of the world, all I could think about were studies I had read that concluded that children of parents who suicided were more likely to suicide. So I sat and I stared down at the water and the boats in the harbor and the lights of the city and I tried to count how many stories I was up in the air based on the condo towers next to the bridge, and then I chose to live and I put my wallet back in my pocket, and I knew, then, what I wanted to be and I knew, then, my reasons for living: being a loving father who would not devastate his child.

I didn't see him at Christmas that year. I didn't see him at his first birthday. And it took me even longer than that to get sober. And then his sister was born and I had a second reason for living and a commitment not to a child but to children and, not long after that, their mother and I also learned that being good parents meant not doing it together. Because he cried "I've lost my mommy!" when she dropped him off, but before we separated he had been regressing, losing words, speaking less, showing symptoms of being on the autism spectrum, but after we separated he flourished and his words came quickly and he was reading bedtime stories to his sister and I before he was in Grade One. And six months after we had settled into the new routine and I was tickling his back as he fell asleep, he turned to me and said, "When I was at mommy's house, I dreamed about I love you so much." "I like that dream a lot," I said. He sighed the happy sighs he sighs when I rub his back or cuddle him close to me. "I still love you when I go to mommy's house," he said as he fell asleep.

(A few nights later, he told me that he had a dream that I had a dream about fish.)

6

My daughter has always loved cats. Cats have always had mixed feelings about my daughter.

7

BEDTIME CONVERSATION WITH A six-year-old and a four-year-old.

>Me: I love you so much. It makes my heart feel so happy to be here with you.
>
>Him: Oh, this hurts my head.
>
>Me: What hurts your head?
>
>Him: People talking!
>
>Me: Oh . . .
>
>Her: *Rub my back, please!*

One month later.

>Her: I wanted you to rub my back last night.
>
>Me: But I did rub your back until you fell asleep.
>
>Her: But I want you to still rub my back when I'm sleeping!

8

I.

I WAS IN COLLECTING a detailed account history of my once joint bank account when the banker told me her daughter had died. She had been staying in the psych ward but they let her out on a day pass and she killed herself. We were approaching the anniversary date. I haven't really gotten over it, she said, and she spoke in a perplexed way, like a mother might, trying to understand how to "get over" the suicide of her daughter, her baby who was dead and gone and no longer there and who, in the midst of some kind of illness and darkness and sorrow, chose that.

    I don't always think it is useful to talk about suicide as a choice (although sometimes I think it is). I think some who suicide were murdered years before they actually stopped living. I didn't say this to my banker, as she was printing off the details of my account so that I could provide them as evidence in Family Court. But I did mention a young Indigenous man I knew who did the same thing on a day pass once, many years ago, although I didn't mention that he hung himself from a door handle with his belt, sitting on the floor, able at any moment to stand up, to untie himself, to walk back out of the bathroom, but he never did and he sat there with a belt around his neck and I think he must have really wanted to die. I don't begrudge him that. People had done horrible things to him and with him. Instead, I talked about sorrows that we always carry, scars we have on our insides, cracks and empty and dark places in our hearts that we learn to live with because they never go away. This seemed to resonate with her. She gave me my papers, complimented me on my children (whom she remembered from another visit to the bank) and I think that was the last time I saw her. Seeing her in public settings, and in interactions with other customers, she looked just fine, like she had it all together, but she was full to overflowing with all that she loved and all that she lost.

At that time, I was also overflowing and broken all to pieces but, somehow, I still walked around like a single entity, a person with arms and legs and jobs and bills that were always paid on time. I was far away from the communities I had sought out for most of my adult life, and I was learning that it is not only people experiencing oppression and poverty and homelessness and colonization who are being called upon to engage in Herculean tasks to just get through the day. It's most of us. People with money and nice jobs and nice houses and nice pictures of nice vacations in nice places on Facebook—they're all just barely holding on as well.

I've been wanting to write about kindness but Mariam Toews was right. It's complicated.[1] Women who are being abused by their intimate partners don't need advice on being more kind, but they do sometimes want assistance getting out and away to somewhere safe. And, given the right set of circumstances, I'm still down with punching Nazis.

II.

I've been thinking a lot about road rage. The other day I saw a woman in a car pull into a lane and not speed up as quickly as the man in the truck behind her would have liked. He tailgated her and then pulled up beside her at a red light. Rolling down his window he screamed terrible things at her. Not that long ago, I saw a woman driver do something similar to another woman. A few months before that, I saw a man in a truck pull out into oncoming traffic, perform a U-turn, and block the left turning lane (boxing in the truck waiting there), so that he could get out of his truck and assault the person now trapped in that vehicle. Road rage is an example of a regular occurrence of what seems to be a massive overreaction—a woman pulls out a little too slowly for the liking of the guy driving down the road behind her and now he is screaming at her you bitch, you cunt, and I think I heard the word hatefuck (what does it say about us that such a word has traction in our culture?) before the guy sped away. The woman looked pretty terrified and frozen, the way I've seen women look when men take off their masks

---

1. See Toews, *A Complicated Kindness*.

and start treating women the way they fantasize about treating them. She reminded me of my mother, many years ago.

But this guy, and that other raging woman, and that other raging guy, I think they're all people who feel like they're already trying to cope with more than they can bear. Add just one more drop of water to their cups, even just the smallest drop, and everything comes spilling out. Please note, I'm not saying this to excuse them or to justify their actions or to say, "hey, those assholes are really the victim in that situation" (because they're not). I'm saying this because this seems to be the broader context in which these interactions are taking place. Everyone, including the assholes, is barely surviving the day and feeling they can't take it anymore. And when you (rightly or wrongly, whatever that means) feel like you are being shit on all the time, you just might jump at opportunities to shit on others.

But there are alternatives and, as an alternative, I've been trying to cultivate gentleness. I'm learning how to relate to others gently, as best I can in whatever interactions I have. In a context where people are starving from the absence of affection (and I think we are, I think that's our context), the smallest drop of gentleness can prompt what might appear to be overreactions. All it took was a little gentleness—communicated more in tone and body language than anything else—and my banker was telling me about her dead daughter. Although I don't know that her daughter is dead so much as dying again and again, every morning that my banker wakes up to the world where her daughter went out on a day pass and never came back.

III.

Peter Maurin used to speak about creating the kind of society "where it is easier for people to be good."[2] I like this idea. It suggests that the cure for road rage isn't so much meditating more and going to anger management and learning to count to ten, as it is learning to structure our life together in such a way that we are not dependent on cars. Most lifelong pedestrians don't get upset when traffic is flowing a little slower than usual—even when they are passengers in cars. Mostly they're thinking, "hey, I'm still getting where I'm going much faster than usual and with less aches and pains in my knees and feet and hamstrings" (even if they are also secretly missing saying good morning to the river and running their fingertips over the long grasses that grow beside their walking path, and wondering if the snails

2. An oft-repeated refrain in Maurin, *Easy Essays*.

have arrived yet). However, when these lifelong pedestrians are rushing and depending on a car to get them where they need to go—because they have to get there quickly or they will displease a boss or miss an appointment, well, that changes everything. Working bullshit jobs has so taken over the hours of our days that we start trying to cram everything else—including travel time between various locations—into the smallest time slots possible so that we can try to get everything done that we want to do outside of work.[3] So, another cure for road rage is to pay people more for doing less, and giving them enough time to get an adequate number of hours of sleep at night.

IV.

I once tried to cut down on my travel time. I started biking to work instead of walking but I found I wasn't having enough time to transition from the stress of my job to my role as a father with my children. When I got to the school to pick up the kids too soon, I was still stressed out and tired and this could carry over into the rest of the evening. However, when I walked, I found I was better able to make that transition and came to my children much more present and excited and ready to talk and play and cook and clean and do all the things a parent does. I have also observed this in my children. We often have wonderful talks walking to and from school and our home. However, on rare occasions when we have gotten car rides, I have noticed that the kids are more prone to fighting with each other and arguing and poking each other in the eye and often, in the car, there are tears even though such things almost never happen when we are walking. We all need transitional moments as we move between different environments and transitioning well takes time. A world where it is easier for me to be good is a world where I have or take or make or steal the time I need to transition between my job and my family. Beyond that, I think we need to talk about how we work shitty jobs in order to support our children but then these shitty jobs rebound on us and make us shittier parents. Any job that drains you and leaves you not fully attentive to your child at the end of the day is bullshit. Being a better parent doesn't necessarily mean scheduling more activities into your day to improve yourself. It means having the freedom to have more time with your children and having the energy you need to play with them then.

3. See Graeber, *Bullshit Jobs*.

V.

But the personal is also political and this applies to kindness, too. When I was carrying more than I could bear, surviving in a set of circumstances that was completely overwhelming to me, simply because I was too stubborn to not not survive, it was interactions with kind people that were a balm on my wounds. Many of these kind people were children—my nephews and nieces and my own kids who would all play with me as if I were someone special and lovely and exciting to play with. To them, I was all of these things and with them I was all those things. But sometimes adults were kind to me, too. And in those interactions, I felt okay. For someone accustomed to feeling constantly not okay, and much worse than that, too, it's hard to describe how wonderful a gift that was to receive from others. Increasingly, it seems that people don't get this feeling from others—they get it from antidepressants or alcohol or pot or hydros or whatever else they can put into their bodies to alter their brain chemistry. If you have a doctor help you do this, you're a good person. If you discover that doctors won't help you in the way that you need and you find your own way to do this, you're a community health concern.

But what I mean to say is that I think the default position for our interactions with strangers or in public and professional environments shouldn't just be politeness and professionalism and a strict adherence to whatever rules, laws, or protocols govern the spaces we inhabit. I think the default position we take should be one of kindness and of gentleness. I'd like that a lot. And when kindness and gentleness conflict with rules and laws and protocols, as they inevitably do, especially in so-called caring professions designed to surveil and discipline members of populations considered deviant (i.e. sick), then I think kindness and gentleness take precedence.

It is Life, not the Rule of Law, that is sacred, and we're all in over our heads.

VI.

I once had a former corrections officer who had been hired at a shelter ask me what kind of punishment I mete out to individuals who "intimidate staff" in the program I help facilitate. I laughed and said it's not something we punish people for since we don't get intimidated. Then I felt like that was a bit of a macho dick move, and I explained that although circumstances that prompt a fear reaction can arise, we don't relate to people as things to be feared but as people to be loved and respected and honored. He didn't quite know what to make of that. I'm pretty sure he has PTSD from his last job.

I've heard a lot of bosses talk about how people are too institutionalized to be treated like real human beings, too institutionalized to be treated with kindness and gentleness and respect and love and affection, but I think the most institutionalized people of all are the staff members who choose to show up every day to work in those institutions. Prisoners don't have much of a choice about staying in prison—guards and bosses, though, they choose to be there and they're the ones who are responsible for how the space is managed and what kind of interactions are normalized therein. They're also the ones who sometimes make me wonder if they've been institutionalized beyond the point of no return. So, if we want a world where it is easier for guards to be good and bosses to be de-institutionalized, then we need to start tearing down prisons. And the same goes for cops and social workers.

This also speaks to the broader point that Men's Rights Activists are missing. If they want to do something about the violence experienced by boys and men, they shouldn't be targeting feminism—they need to be targeting patriarchy. Jennifer Newsom and bell hooks have this figured out: the making of men, in our culture, is premised upon the devastation of boys.[4] But, beyond that, if, sometimes, somewhere, a woman beats up her male partner, or a female mother sexually assaults her son, this is not evidence that feminism is violent or destructive or bad. It is evidence that, if you systematically engage in sexual and other forms of violence against girls and women, and do this across the board to everyone for generations, sometimes some people go on to treat others the way they have been treated. MRAs refuse to understand this point and so, instead of deconstructing rape culture (wherein local male university students hang signs from their windows reading "No means yes. And yes means anal." which I've since learned, is not an uncommon chant during frosh weeks across Canada and the USofA), they promote rape apologists and double down on a culture that blames women and promotes violence against women because accepting some kind of notion of male guilt or culpability seems to be more than they can bear.

---

4. See hooks, *The Will to Change*; and Newsom, *The Mask You Live In*. See also, Kimmel, *Angry White Men*.

Why is this the case? I have been fortunate enough to know several good men over the course of my life—men who acknowledge the ways in which they benefit from patriarchy and men who are working hard to fight against it. These are men who understand that accepting responsibility within an androcentric and patriarchal society is not a thing that diminishes them but, instead, is something that liberates them. These are men who seem to be okay with the idea that they have to do things to improve themselves and that improvement of this sort, in this context, is a lifelong project.

I think most men recoil from this because they feel like they're already in over their heads and dealing with more than they can bear. They don't want improvement, they want succor. Which, of course, means that when they look to women to mother them or fuck them (since men are not encouraged to soothe and comfort one another), and women refuse to play these roles (Porphyria R'lyeh, on a tumblr page that no longer exists: "women are not machines you put kindness coins into until sex falls out"), these men lay all the blame on women.

Which also means, I think, that if I want to do something about patriarchy I, as a man, should be cautious about demonizing other men and should, instead, try, as a man, to find ways to offer succor to other men. This means avoiding the general ways that men do this with other men (talking about how all women are bitches, excusing or valorizing acts of violence, or engaging in social activities that provide people with the opportunity to experience themselves performing macho-ness), and opening a space where men can comfort other men in an anti-patriarchal, feminist manner. Maybe then the absolutely necessary improvements become a possibility.

And I'm not saying this is right or as it should be, but I am trying to think about what tactics might produce what results. And engaging on this front does not negate other engagements elsewhere. I'm a fan of a diversity of tactics. And if a patriarchal world is structured in such a way as to produce men who are overly sensitive to criticism and incapable of coping well with guilt or responsibility, then this, too, is one of the structures of patriarchy that must be torn down. Engaging in this task needn't be a misplaced focus of energy, as if one is making the sufferings of men more important than the women and children who suffer at the hands of men. If male violence is the problem, then we've got to do something about men and, it seems to me, men are well situated to be allies to women by choosing to engage with violent men and with the structures that make it difficult for these men to be engaged. It makes good sense as Malcolm pointed out all those years ago that white people should go deal with white people; white people should go deal with white people, and men should go deal with men.

It's the same tactic I use when working with men who have sexually abused children and who have been classified as highly likely to reoffend when released to the community. When such men come into my work, I try very hard to be safe, welcoming, and useful to them. I try to be kind and form a therapeutic rapport. Some people would argue this kindness is a betrayal of the children these men have harmed, some people would argue that these men should be killed, but they are not killed and I am not going to kill them, and, given this context, they are more likely to reoffend if they are ostracized and treated like monsters but less likely to reoffend if they develop positive relationships in the community. So, who benefits the most from me trying to create this? Well, to my mind, the children who don't end up being abused if this ends up working.

VII.

I have been thinking about the term "gentleman" and what a good thing it is to aspire to be and what a shame it is that the term was co-opted by a rapacious and parasitical upper class (as if being a gentleman has to do with the softness of one's hands, the cleanness of one's clothes, and the odor of one's armpits, and nothing at all to do with treating the lives and bodies and sex of "those less fortunate" as completely disposable).

VIII.

For the last two years of our marriage, I was not a good husband to my wife. I did not know how to deal with conflict, especially when it was very intense and feelings were very escalated. I did not know what to do with strong feelings of anger or frustration or hurt. When my father had shown strong feelings in our household when I was a child, it was terrifying and frequently resulted in physical violence. Often this was hard to foresee. Outbursts came suddenly and seemingly at random (he, too, probably felt like he had been given more than he could bear in life). So, it went for the familial conflicts I had experienced and I knew I did not want to be like him. Consequently, the stronger my feelings, the more I shut down. The more intensely angry or frustrated or hurt I felt, the flatter my affect became. I became expressionless, mute, and non-responsive. As a result of this, my wife often became more escalated and so we fell into a spiral where our reactions were triggers to each other. I became more withdrawn as she became more escalated, and she became more escalated as I became more withdrawn, until I finally physically withdrew from the situation and went off to the local pub to drink with other men—the regulars—who, as they got to know me, complained about their exes and showed me pictures of kids they hadn't seen in years.

It would have been easy for me to then present myself as a victim in that situation, to present my wife and her way of dealing with conflict in the worst possible light, while presenting myself as a silent and long-suffering victim, but the truth was that my way of dealing with conflict was just as fucked as hers.

It took me a long time to realize this and I regret that I did not realize this about myself sooner. Because not knowing how to deal with a situation is not an excuse for not learning how to deal with it well. At that time, I found some comfort with those men at the pub. But I am beginning to think if we rely on anything too long for comfort, it starts to play against us. I see this all the time with people who turn to substances for relief, but who end up in relationships of long-term dependency that end up stealing everything else from their lives. This doesn't just apply to dependencies upon substances which have been made illicit (thereby causing a whole host of other barriers and harms to enter into a person's life). It's everywhere. It's in our relationships and in shopping malls and places of worship and academic institutions and social media.

Eventually, perhaps, we need to move beyond being comforted to being okay. Okay-ness sometimes means learning to carry inside of ourselves parts that can never be comforted. I came to a point when I learned I did not have to try and fill my wounds and empty places with things to distract me from them. Instead, I learned to live with them inside of me. I learned that these wounds and holes and broken pieces were a part of me and I accepted them as such. I have also learned other ways of negotiating conflict. If I am upset about something, I have learned to contextualize my feelings and communicate them. I will say, "It hurt my feelings when you did this thing . . . but I don't know if that's because what you did was hurtful in and of itself or because I am carrying sensitivities forward from previous relationships where I experienced this other thing, so can we talk about this together and see where that takes us?" At first I felt a bit silly or immature talking this way because it sounds so childlike (i.e. childish) but I have learned that the

The Second Part: Father

wisdom of children often far exceeds the maturity of men and the silliness of children is more life-giving than the seriousness of adults and the love of children transforms us into who we long to be because, to children, unless we prove them wrong, we already are good, we already are special, we already are a delight to be with, and we already are beloved. And what I often think is the deepest wound of all in men is that they have proved their children wrong and until we find ways to create spaces where men can confront that about themselves, we are, all of us, doomed.

9

Her, 4 years old: Let's play mommies and daddies.

Me: How do we play that?

Her: First we go to work, then we go to sleep. Sometimes we kitchen.

10

Me: What did I say is the most important thing?

Him, 7 years old: Being good and obeying all the rules?

Me, somewhat horrified: What? No! Being kind—being kind is the most important thing and sometimes we have to break the rules to be kind.

11

It was the morning of July 1st, 2015, it was a Wednesday, when my kids' mom agreed to settle our case before going to trial.

It was in the afternoon of July 30th, 2015, it was a Thursday, when she and her lawyer actually signed the papers with us and agreed to the terms put forward by my lawyer and I.

It was November 5th, 2015, another Thursday, when I received the Final Order from the Judge, which made everything official. I was divorced, I was a father, and I was grateful.

Dates are easy to list. I was served August 1st, 2014, sitting at my desk at work, my hands shaking, vomit rising in my throat, dread encircling me. I was married on March 3rd, 2007, dancing and laughing and struggling to contain my tears when the woman who would be my wife began to walk towards me down the aisle. She was beautiful and we were young and vulnerable and we didn't know what we were doing.

Dates are easy to list, it's everything else that is hard to think, to speak, to communicate.

My wife tried to take my kids away from me, she tried to get them to call another man dad instead of me, she tried to get the Court to order the children into her custody based on a fabricated narrative—but how can I speak about that in a way that does her justice and that still acknowledges the ways in which I hurt her and our relationship? How can I speak about sitting before a Judge while my wife's lawyer does everything she can to make me appear that I am unfit to be a parent, to make it appear, in fact, like I am already not being a parent, to make it appear that her sole motivation is the best interest of the children and, based upon the story she is telling, that means getting rid of me? At that stage in the Family Court process, no evidence was required to back up those statements—what was required was that I sit silently, calmly, still. And I did. And I won the Court case

The Second Part: Father

and, on the morning of July 1st, 2015, I knew once and for all that never, never, never could my children be taken from me. And walking home from the Courthouse I intermittently laughed and cried and shouted for joy and when I got home I fell on my knees and hugged my children and the tears poured out of me and my chest shook with sobs and they asked me, "Daddy, why are you crying?" and I said to them, "I am crying because I am so glad to be your daddy and sometimes, when we feel a very big kind of love and a very deep kind of happiness, we cry in the same way as when we feel a very big sorrow or a very deep hurt." And so they hugged me back and said they loved me very big, too.

What did my lawyer and I ask for? Only that both parents would have equal time with their children, that both parents would be involved in decisions related to education and medical care, and that neither parent would be able to unilaterally remove the children from the community where they had put down roots and where they were thriving and growing. And, just in case that makes it look like I'm trying to come off as a good guy suffering at the hands of a villainous wife, it should be recalled that there were nights when I was out drinking with my lover and she was at home with a baby with colic and she would call me for help and I would turn off my phone.

12

I was swatting flies when he pulled on my arm, he is seven now, and said, "Daddy, why are you killing flies? They're living nature." And then I wasn't swatting flies anymore.

13

Her, 4½ years old and standing on her tippy toes: Look, daddy, I'm a giant!

14

I.

Dear Children,

It is the end of 2015. One of you is four and one-half years old. The other of you is almost seven. I was looking back over a lot of old photos (and new ones, too) and I realized that, wow, we have really been building a life together. How 'bout that, eh? The years are flying by and you are becoming ever more alive and wonderful, as your bodies and hearts and minds and personalities continue to grow. And me? In some ways I feel like I am becoming smaller—but not in a bad way. Perhaps I am becoming more concentrated. More concentrated and more content. It's not something that bothers me. In fact, I feel grateful for it.

A lot has happened over this year. Most of it, I have forgotten already. Running errands, filling out forms at work, packing lunches, going to meetings, brushing teeth and changing bed sheets—all the thousands of things that fill up days that come and go and are forgotten almost as quickly as they happen. But some things I have not forgotten. Legal matters between your mother and I were settled. And I learned and now believe—with as much certainty as any of us can have about anything in lives that are so fragile—that no one was or is going to be able to separate us. Not now, at least. Not this way. We will continue to be together and barring any unforeseeable tragedy (and I have done the work I do for far too long to think anyone is exempt from unforeseeable tragedies), we will continue to be together for a long time yet.

Well, for you it may feel like a long time. For me, it seems to be passing faster than I can catch my breath. The babies who fit on my palm and wrist turned into toddlers, and the toddlers who slept on shelves and in baskets have turned into children. And me? I'm a middle-aged man who has gotten old and turned into a father. It all happened so quickly. I breathed in, breathed out, took a nap, woke up, and here we all are. Son, Daughter, Daddy.

II.

My own father wasn't a very kind father. I think his insides, like his heart and mind and that part inside of us that makes us tangibly care about other people as people who are breathtaking and sacred and fragile and valuable, well, I think those inside parts in my father got deformed. Or, perhaps better said, I think they were prevented from forming and maturing because of what he experienced as a child. The violence of his parents got into his insides and messed them up, but that violence also took root inside of him and grew up along with him. So, as an adult and a father, he was broken and self-absorbed and violent and, to me, he was terrifying.

Sometimes, thinking about my childhood makes me sad. In fact, the other day, I found myself saying, "I wish that I had a father who loved me as a child," by which I really mean "a father who was kind to me." Because, of course, my father will say that he loved me, and my brothers, and my mom, very much—how he wept when she finally left him—but he is mistaking a feeling for an action and, really, what matters is love in action (and love in action is kind, even if kindness sometimes take surprising forms). I was surprised to hear myself saying this. Ever since I was kicked out by my parents eighteen years ago, I have always said that I didn't need any mother or father or any substitute mother—or father-figure in my life. Friends, guides, mentors, companions, and lovers? Sure, absolutely I wanted and needed people like that in my life. But fathers or mothers? No, thanks.

So, I was surprised to find myself saying these things and feeling this way. I think being a father who knows lovingkindness (that's an old word but it says so much so well!) and experiencing all the joy and wonder that comes with that has opened me to mourning some things in new ways. As I write this, I am not angry that my father's love did not know kindness, but I am sad about it. Sad like the way I feel sad about friends who have died over the years.

You don't yet know this kind of sadness but when people we love die, we continue to live—and we can continue to feel joy and peace and excitement—but there are parts inside of us that remain quiet and empty and sad and sometimes, even feel that way when all the other parts of us are laughing and feeling playful. And that's okay. It's okay to have quiet and empty

A Magnificent Work

and sad parts and it's okay to cry, too—it's good to mourn those we love who are parted from us and it's okay to honor them with our tears—and I think I have sometimes suppressed my mourning rather than allow myself to feel it.

Sometimes we do this when the things that make us sad feel so big that we think maybe they are bigger than we are and maybe they will overwhelm us. I think the murder of my own childhood felt that way to me and, although I have often revisited it over the years, I sometimes still find little forgotten pieces buried deep inside myself. This thought, "I wish I had a father who loved me [who was kind to me] when I was a child" was one of those pieces. And so I've pulled it out and I mourn it now. Doing this is a good way to stop the violence of others—the violence they inflict upon us, although you don't know too much about any of that yet—from taking root inside of us and from growing in us the way the violence of my grandparents grew inside my father. I think maybe when he was a child, he never had anybody with whom he could share his sadness. I mourn this, too. And so, one of the things I have tried to be in life, is a person with whom others can share their sadness. It's not always easy being a repository of sorrows but, if you can bear up under it, you will bring a lot of love and hope and comfort into the lives of others. When you think about what you want to be when you grow up, I would like to encourage you to consider being this sort of person as well.

Because when you think about what you want to be when you grow up, I hope you define yourself less by what job you want to do (or, more literally, how you trade your labor for money) and more by the kind of person you want to be in relation to others. Son, I know you want to be a chef when you grow up. That's a lot of fun and Daughter and I have been enjoying cooking and baking with you, but when I think about what I hope for you and Daughter, what I hope is that you will want to be people who engage with others (and by others I don't just mean other people, I also mean the trees, and the river, and the land) with lovingkindness. This is not the case of a member of an older generation (me) expecting or desiring that the younger generation (you two) to succeed where I have not—as so often happens with matters related to the environment, poverty, war, disease and justice. The older generations mess up the world for their own profit and then expect the younger ones to fix it which, itself, is an injustice and an expression of selfishness. This is not what I am expressing here. I am committed to showing you the way of lovingkindness. Whether or not you will be loving, and kind, and the sort of people with whom others share their sorrows and find at least a little comfort and companionship, will have a lot to do with whether or not I embody these things not only in my relationship with you two but also with everyone else (including the trees, and the river, and the land).

III.

You still make me laugh uproariously.

> Her: Are we real?
>
> Me: Yes, we are real.
>
> Her: Am I real? Are you? Is my brother real?
>
> Me: Yes, you are real, I am real, and your brother is real.
>
> Him: Your face smells like beard.
>
> Me: My face smells like what?
>
> Him: Like beard!
>
> Her: I want a pet monkey.
>
> Me: What the heck is happening right now?
>
> Her: A pet space monkey!

III.

Recently, my father said that he wished that he had been less scary—because then his kids would have approached him more and learned that he loved them more than they knew. His voice cracked when he said this, but it was hard to know if he was feeling sorrow for his children or was only feeling sorry for himself. It was probably some combination of the two. But it doesn't matter. It really doesn't. Feelings cannot change the past and this is one of the parts that was broken inside of me as a child: the ability to feel intimacy with my parents. I try and I try, and I visit them, and try to be sensitive to their needs, and work on loving them (by which I am referring to the actions I take in relation to them) in a way that they experience as loving, but inside of me things don't connect.

    I've often said that our insides are like our outsides—when our skin is cut it can heal but sometimes it leaves a scar, when we break a leg or ankle the bones can heal but we can end up limping, and sometimes—if a finger gets frostbite or a toe gets gangrene—a part of our outsides is removed in order to make sure the rest of our body continues to live. And it does. Our bodies, the bodies that we are, continue to live but they have scars and limps and missing parts. I think our insides are the same. Our hearts can get cut, heal and scar, or break and heal but limp. And sometimes, too, parts of a heart get cut out to prevent the rest of the heart from dying. And this is what I've learned with my own parents—I am better able to love them in the ways in which they desire to be loved, as long as I don't look for them to produce a feeling inside of me that feels like the feeling of "being loved."

This probably doesn't make much sense to you now and I wish, I wish, I wish, it never will make sense to you but it is probably inevitable that one day when you are older you will know exactly what I'm talking about because you will feel it inside yourselves. Even the best of daddies cannot prevent his children from getting their hearts broken at some point. That is beyond what I can do. But I can be safe and loving place for you now and continue to be that kind of place for you so that when that time comes perhaps I can help you through it.

IV.

> Her: I have a surprise for you.
>
> Me: You do?
>
> Her: Yep, it's beautiful!
>
> Me: It is?
>
> Her: Yepperdoodles! Soooo beautiful! It's so beautiful it will make your eyes burn!
>
> Me: Oh my gosh . . . um . . . what is it?
>
> Her, looking side to side then whispering in my ear: *It's chips!*

V.

My own father terrified me but I have categorically refused any kind of fear-based methods to parenting (a lot of what people refer to as "disciplining" their kids is really just teaching their kids to fear them in order to make the kids do what they want them to do—and no matter how widely accepted this is, I maintain that it is fucked up), because I want you to know, in both your minds and your bodies, that you are safe with me. I can't make the whole world safe—I wish I could but this, too, is beyond me—but I can make myself a safe person. You can rely on me for this.

Because this is another important thing to know—as much as it is nice to be the kind of person who loves and cares for others, you will also experience times when you need the love and care of others. In fact, we all experience that all the time. You are just unconscious of that need right now. When you become aware of it, don't run from it. Accept it. There is no shame in allowing those who love you to carry you in times of need. One day when I am very old, if I get to be very old, you may carry me, too.

VI.

This is another of the things I have not forgotten from 2015: At night we often watch a short cartoon together before bedtime. We sit on the love seat in your room, her on one side of me, him on the other, and we cuddle up together. You are often sleepy, especially her, and you relax into me. She rests her head on my forearm and he nuzzles up on my chest with his head under my chin. I can feel both of you breathing. I can smell your hair. My arms are around both of you and I
    am
    content.

15

IN THE BOAT AT the bottom of Niagara Falls, he is eight and he is in my arms against the front railing and we are absolutely soaked from the spray and he is laughing and squealing and everything about him embodies that unselfconscious way in which children can express joy. Later, after visiting the Butterfly Conservatory, where his gestures expressed a muted awe and a barely contained wonder, I ask him, "What was your favorite part of the trip?" and he replies, "Spending time with my family."

16

Her, five years old: When are you going to take us to Disneyland?

Me: Disneyland?? That's a lot of money.

Her: You should just work and work and work and work and then when you're a hundred you can take us.

Me: That seems about right.

17

Last week, my daughter brought home a bottle full of worms she had collected in the playground. She talks to them and says that they can hear her. She says she understands them, too, because she can speak their language. I ask her what they say and I remember, when I was a very little boy, how the stray dogs came and lay down at my feet, and so when she tells me what they say, I believe her.

My daughter is six years old today. She tells me she loves me, in part, because, like her, I love "all the animals." But when I dumped the worms out in the yard after she went to bed, and tried to tell them to get while the getting was good, I don't think they understood me.

Sometimes my daughter sees things that other people don't see. Deer playing on the edge of a farmer's field, "It's a mother and a baby," she says, "I'm seeing them with my special eyes." Sometimes she takes me by the cheeks and stares into my eyes with those special eyes of hers . . . and then sticks her tongue up my nose and laughs and laughs at my reaction. She still writes a lot of letters backwards and sometimes mixes up her 6s and 9s but she paints beautiful pictures on paper and canvas and my face and she cried when she accidentally broke a branch on a tree (because she loves the trees and doesn't want to hurt them). She is attentive to her friends and wants them to be as happy as she is. She's kind and she's good and she's innocent and will play with you endlessly ("I only watch movies when I'm bored because nobody will play with me"). But, no matter how I try, I can't capture her in words. She's a mystery and a wonder and a miracle. She's holier than god.

God, after all, is only as holy as the most profane among us. God is as holy as a father is when he is putting out his cigarette on the inner thigh of his fourteen-year-old daughter. I knew that daughter and I saw the scars that were left behind, and now I am a father and I have a daughter whose

The Second Part: Father

middle name is "Beloved" (Toni Morrison: "In the dark my name is Beloved") and I don't want much of anything to do with gods and the men of violence they inspire.[1]

How can a child make sense of such violence? Children are so full of love for their parents, even the most abusive parents, that they blame themselves for it. They make sense of their abuse by telling themselves, "I'm not good enough, I must be bad or broken; I've done something to deserve this." They can live in terror every day but still, love comes so naturally to them, that they love the ones terrorizing them and, instead of blaming their abusers or thinking their abusers are bad or broken, they choose to believe the worst kinds of things about themselves. In this way, it is not only the sins of the fathers that are visited upon their children. The children also carry the sense of guilt of the fathers. And so abusers walk through life feeling justified while abuse survivors walk through life feeling like they are to blame for everything. A lot of people end up with a lifetime of self-loathing mitigated by substance use because they will not, 'til the day they die, believe that their parents simply chose, for no good reason at all, to repeatedly do horrendous things to them. They find it easier to believe horrible things about themselves, even as adults (and then they go on to act in ways that reinforce that belief) because they loved their abusers too deeply when they were children and never learned to love themselves (because they were doing all the loving and not receiving any back).

I had to process some of these things myself and, although I began to know myself as beloved quite some time ago, it wasn't until having children of my own that I realized what a miracle and gift I was when I was brand new. It wasn't until I held my own babies in my arms that I realized, no, I never once did a thing to deserve the way I was treated. Not even a little bit. Not at all. Not a single goddamn thing. And I sometimes wonder if Christians hold onto a doctrine of original sin and the belief that all of us are born worthy of damnation in order to justify the things they do to their kids. Woe to you, parents, who steal what can never be returned, and who, instead of becoming like little children, take little children and make them into your own image.

My daughter is her own. I sometimes refer to her as my daughter or my child but she isn't mine. If anything, it's the other way around. She is learning to fly and I am her nest, a big ol' tree with knots and missing branches, but her tree nonetheless, where she can always come and feel safe

---

1. Morrison, *Beloved*, 75. And see also, Nouwen, *Life of the Beloved*.

A Magnificent Work

and happy and at home. And though she loves my scars and knows where to tickle me, although she adores me and laughs at all the ways she can bend me without breaking me, I won't make her into my own image. She is her own image.

And, darling, today is your birthday and I am trying to write you a love letter that captures something of the love and wonder and gratitude I feel because you are in my life, but I trip over the words and I stumble and I erase what I wrote because, even though you are still teeny tiny, all that is in you is bigger and fuller and better than any combination of words I can write. I love you, darling. Happy birthday.

18

Him, 8 years old: I think the Easter bunny is you. Because you look very white in darkness. And also, you're pretty hairy. So, I think the Easter bunny is you. And Santa Claus. And also, I think, a leprechaun! [He then tries to pull my face off to reveal the leprechaun underneath.]

19

I.

It is Christmas, 2016. My children are opening gifts, dancing, being silly, and laughing. Abruptly, my daughter pauses and asks me, "Why are there no presents for you under the tree?" and before I can answer my son says, "Because all he ever wants are hugs and kisses." And then they jump on me and hug me and kiss me and roll me on the floor with them and it is all that I have ever wanted.

II.

I had to learn how to be a father. My father didn't teach me, and I grew up in a very controlled environment, which, looking back on it now, feels like a deliberately enforced isolation, almost an imprisonment, wherein I had little opportunity to witness other men acting as good fathers because I was very rarely permitted to go to the homes of friends, in part, because I was very rarely permitted to have friends.

By the time I got to high school, I didn't really know how to socialize. I didn't know how to talk with my peers. I didn't know how to overcome the shyness that debilitated me and, apart from extravagant acts of recklessness that got me pegged as the crazy punk rock kid (which, thankfully, led bullies to leave me alone as they went on to target other shy, geeky kids who didn't fit in and who hadn't figured out how to put on a persona that covered over their vulnerabilities), I mostly found myself standing by awkwardly while others talked, never sure when to intervene, never sure why anyone would want to listen to me anyway, but never sure when to walk away. Later, when I was kicked out by my father, three of my closest friends were also being kicked out by their parents on a semi-regular basis. One

The Second Part: Father

finally fought back, another had a dad who had vanished years before, and the third was constantly clashing with his mom's asshole boyfriends. So, we learned to survive on our own. I wanted to prove that I didn't need a father or a parent or anyone else. I finished high school while working late shifts at a fast food joint, I went to college, I aced my courses, and I spoke as the valedictorian. My mother came to the ceremony. My father didn't.

Friend, companion, lover, ally, co-conspirator, partner, community member, these were the kinds of relationships I pursued. Along the way, I encountered some male guides and men who inspired and believed in me and helped shape and transform me, but I never once thought of them as father figures. And I laughed at friends who, in their twenties, still called their parents when it came time to make simple decisions. I thought there was something wrong with them.

So, I had to learn how to be a father and, at first, I wasn't sure if I was going to. I had been pursuing a career within social services that was deeply connected to my own values and to the identity I wanted to pursue for myself, but I became increasingly convinced that social services actually normalized abusive practices targeting the people whom they claimed to serve. Social services were, in fact, a part of the problems they claimed they were working to solve. They reinforced narratives that perpetuated and further deepened systems and structures of oppression, poverty, and violence, while also contributing to those systems and structures. Therefore, I increasingly tried to pursue non-professional relationships, neighborliness, and personal friendships with those who experience oppression, poverty, and violence while also engaging in communal acts of solidarity, resistance and liberation. However, as Real Estate Developers, with the full complicity of City Hall and the Police, slowly took over Vancouver's downtown eastside, the neighborhood I called home (and a land they described as terra nullius, harkening back to old colonial lies perpetuating the ongoing theft of land), I found myself increasingly driven to the conclusion that those intent on hoarding wealth stolen from the land, bodies, health, children, and lives of those whom they oppress were actually winning on every front. Therefore, I became increasingly convinced that an act of radical violence may be the only thing that might reorient the map, upset the balance of power, and make possible things that, hitherto, were not possible. If victory is not possible, then instead of constantly fighting battles that we lose, we need to change the conditions in which we fight so that victory becomes possible. An act of revolutionary violence seemed like it might be able to do this.

A Magnificent Work

As I wondered these things, I also found myself with a steadily decreasing desire to live. Everything was coming apart—my marriage, the community of which I had been a part, my understanding of myself and what I would or would not do, my understanding of the world—and I was weary, weary, weary of the patriarchal, colonial, heteronormative, and class-based violence that was the ubiquitous experience of those whom I loved. Bodies scarred, hearts broken, marked and unmarked graves, we were losing and I was increasingly convinced that we would lose entirely if someone didn't risk everything in the kind of act that one can only take once.

And then my son was born.

III.

It is springtime. 2017. We are walking home from school together. My son is 8 and my daughter is 6. We are all holding hands. I am in the middle carrying their backpacks on my back. It is not so much to carry and it is much easier then when I carried them, in snowsuits wrapped in blankets to school and daycare in the brutally cold winters of 2013 and 2014. I caught pneumonia then, sweating through t-shirts and sweaters carrying them and then walking to work afterwards, but I didn't have much of a choice about it.

> Him: Why did god create violence?
>
> Me: Ummmm...
>
> Him: Because god is good, right? And cares about us? So why did god create violence?
>
> Me: Ummmm...
>
> Him: I think maybe god is a little bit not nice. And that's the part of god that made violence.
>
> Me: Where are you getting all these ideas about god?
>
> Him: I just make them up.
>
> Me: Ah yes, well, there is a very long tradition of people doing that.
>
> Her: God is also the earth.
>
> Him: Yeah, and trees are god reaching up from the earth to hug us.
>
> Her: Trees have names.
>
> Me: If you hug trees it helps you feel good. Try it!

The Second Part: Father

>Her, hugging a tree: It's pointy!
>
>Me: Don't hug the pointy parts!

IV.

My son was born when I was straddling the worlds of the living and the dead. I no longer wanted to live but I felt that dying was impermissible. I was, I thought, in every way, superfluous. I did not think my son needed me—how many of us grow up fatherless, I asked myself and, not only that, but how many of us wish that we had grown up fatherless? So, I sought permission to die, but as I searched through study after study, I consistently found that children of fathers who suicide are more likely to suicide. I didn't want my son to suicide. I didn't want him to be more likely to suicide. And so I drank. And drinking was a form of living and drinking was a form of dying. Laughing and singing and fighting and fucking. And then regaining consciousness in a doorway with shit in my pants and puke in my hair and walking home to take a shower and take over looking after my son so that my wife could get some rest after a sleepless night of a crying baby and unanswered phone calls.

I had a lot to learn. I had to learn how to be a father but, more than that, I had to relearn how to be a good man, I had to be honest with myself about myself, I had to give up a good many things—not just smoking and drinking but also hopes and dreams and a whole identity—and I had to be content with that. The birth of my son made me a father. But I did not become a good father until I, too, was born again.

V.

Walking home from school a few months later.

>Her: Where is god?
>
>Me: Wha..?! Ummm . . . that's a question a lot of people have asked for a long time.
>
>Her: Where is god?
>
>Me: Um . . . do you ever talk with god?
>
>Her: Yep!
>
>Me: And does god talk with you?

A Magnificent Work

Her: Yep!

Me: What do you talk about?

Her: The earth. Because god is the earth.

VI.

I was startled when my children started talking with me about god. I did not engage in god-talk with them. Because god was one of the things I had given up. I know they weren't getting this talk from their mother. And the gal who loves me, and whom I love, and with whom I first understood the notion of being *in* love, she also doesn't believe in god. She never has. She went through more than any child should ever have to go through, as many children do. I played her a song about a child who died and the singer asks why wasn't god watching, why wasn't god there, for this girl, and the singer imagines the girl, young and full of trust and laughter and playfulness, and she died, she was taken, her body was found beside a highway, and the singer asks why and why and why, and this gal I know who doesn't believe in god, this gal who has never believed in god, broke down and cried while she listened.

God is such a lovely story. And it seems that most of us look back on moments when we lost our innocence, when parts on the outside and inside of us were broken or taken and at least some part of us wishes that we had been protected from that moment that someone, something, anything, god, whatever, had been there because we were young and we were innocent and we were full of trust and laughter and playfulness and part of us died, and was taken, and we were left behind, alone, undone. It would have been lovely to have been saved from all that. Gods and salvation and happy endings, these are such seductive ideas.

VII.

Last night, I sat with my daughter in my arms and played video games with my son (my daughter played too, holding a controller for a radio-controlled car and yelling "Unbeatable!" and "Undefeated!" while randomly pressing buttons). At bedtime they sat in my lap while I read a story. I tucked them in and then sat beside my daughter's bed and rubbed her back until she fell asleep (I always do this, and people always say something like, "oh, that's so sweet!", but if I don't do it, she won't go to sleep and is constantly in and out of bed). She fell asleep quickly and I stood up and stroked my son's forehead and cheeks (he's in the top bunk) and ran my fingers through his hair. He rolled over so that he was closer to me and smiled with his eyes closed and then he fell asleep, too.

I've given up on trying to sing to them because my daughter always tells me to be quiet and covers her ears (she has done this ever since she was a baby in the crib—I first remember her doing this when she was 1½ years old, placing her hand over my mouth and saying, "Shhh"). Instead, I tell them that I love them and that they are beautiful and that they are smart and strong and brave and wonderful and make my heart feel so happy—so happy that sometimes it feels like it is going to burst out of my chest. I spend a lot of time telling them that they are good. It may seem like an odd thing to repeat, "you're such a good girl, you're such a good boy," but it took me more than thirty years to shake the sense of guilt that was planted in me as a child and I don't want them carrying that. Children need to know that they are good.

VIII.

A couple of days ago the national news was all over a story about how a former high-level manager for the Ministry of Children and Family Development, who was also a director for the British Colombia Youth in Care Network (a foster parent himself) had been arrested for possessing child pornography. I knew this man. During the last year or so of my time working for a shelter and residential living program for street-involved youth in Vancouver, he was hired on as an Assistant Program Manager. He was a prick but that's pretty par for the course when it comes to the highest paid Senior Managers within the non-profit industrial complex. He was smart and manipulative and was very talented at working people to his side and his advantage. I guess those are skills you want to learn if you're a Senior Manager or a child pornographer. As the story developed, it came to light that he did more to kids than look at pictures.

I don't ask why to god about this sort of thing anymore. If there is any god out there, responsible for creating all of this, then all that can be said of us is that we have all been betrayed. We have all been abandoned.

It's not that anyone I know has a problem with the idea of a justice and peace and love kind of god. A god who can heal all wounds, wipe away all tears, and make all things new? A god who can bring about shalom? Sure, I'll take four, please. Oh, wait, this god doesn't seem to be doing much of anything tangible for anyone around these parts? Oh, wait, "the family that prays together still probably dies in the fire." No point in waiting around here then, especially given all that other things god is used for. And if that kind of justice and peace and love and healing god shows up, well, what did Heine say? "God will forgive me; that's his [sic] job."

But, wait, who wants to be forgiven by a god who has abandoned us? That seems a little backwards to me. Any god who shows up proclaiming, "I forgive you!" is no better than a father who abandons his children in the middle of a war zone and then comes back thirty years later saying, "I forgive you!"

Fuck that guy.

IX.

My daughter likes me to take her by the hands and spin her around when we dance. I painted her nails for her the other day and she was so excited that she gave me a giant hug—lifting her legs off the floor and kicking them back behind her, like we were in a cheesy movie and I was her long lost father and we finally found each other at a remote airport in Indonesia in the rain. She is most ticklish on her legs just above her knees. Her laughter is pure laughter and when I laugh with her

    mine

    is

    too.

(And what does my son say when we are walking down the sidewalk together and he is holding his sister's hand and I tell them how much joy they bring me? "Yeah, I make your heart feel better and you make my heart feel better.")

When I walk down the street with her and my son in my arms, or with one on either side of me, holding my hands, I may grumble about how much they weigh, or I may complain about my bad knees, or the snow in the air and the ice on the sidewalk, but really in my heart I know that I am the luckiest fellow in the world. And I don't need a god to know that I am blessed and that each one of us is sacred and that the earth we walk upon is holy ground.

The Second Part: Father

X.

In the fall of her sixth year, two months after she had started Senior Kindergarten, my daughter came to the following conclusion about god and the earth: "Everything is alive in the universe. The universe is actually alive. The earth is alive. If the earth is alive, everything is alive." But I think my children only began to contemplate god after they became aware of death. My son first asked me about death one night in May, 2015. He crawled into my bed, well after his bedtime (I thought he had fallen asleep), and, with tears in his eyes, asked me if he was going to die. "Yes, darling, you are going to die." And he asked me if wizards die, and he wasn't sure if they did and then he thought maybe he would like to grow up to be a wizard.

It wasn't until October, 2016, when my daughter came to the same realization. We were driving beside a graveyard and my son asked if people are dead before they were put in the ground or if they died after. My daughter suddenly understood the concept of death. She asked, "Is mommy going to die?" "Yes, mommy is going to die." "Are you going to die?" "Yes, I am going to die." "Is my brother going to die?" "Yes, your brother is going to die." "Is Nana going to die?" "Yes, Nana is going to die." "Am I going to die?" "Yes, everyone dies eventually." And then she was sobbing inconsolably and, through tears and spit and snot she kept up a heartrending cry, "I don't want to die! I don't want mommy to die! I don't want Nana to die! I don't want to die! I don't want to die!"

A few months later, when my son was explaining to me that maybe I was here, in this world, because god gave me life (when I asked him where that idea came from, he said he just knew it), my daughter disagreed and said "god is only after we die" and happily continued on her way to school.

I'm not sure what to make of this god-talk. Longing for a god who never came to save my loved ones, never came to save us, all of us, every single goddamn one of us, left me shattered like a child in Sunday school, his father receiving a message in the sanctuary and getting up and coming downstairs, not to comfort him but to take him out to the van and there . . . and there . . .

And there.

No, I am done with god-talk. If there is such a thing or being or singularity (or whatever word you want to use) as "god," then I imagine this thing is well beyond our language or our concepts. To speak of this, would be ever only to lie (it would be as if the bacteria in my intestinal tract tried to speak of me, of having a personal relationship with me, of me coming to save them . . . only, in this multiverse of space-time in which we are for only the most unimaginably brief moment, I am far, far smaller than a bacterium).

XI.

I took everything I was before, everything I hoped for, everything I dreamed, everything I believed, every conclusion I had come to, and I wrote them into a story, and I categorized them as fiction, and I sent it all to a publisher, and then I walked away.

XII.

I once laughed at friends who used to call their parents for help making what struck me as seemingly minor decisions. Now I am left staggered by the idea that my children, when they are adults, will want to spend time with me and will seek out my advice. I have no frame of reference for this.

After Father's Day this year, my father emailed to complain that I never contacted him. I didn't bother explaining to him that Father's Day is the one day of the year I absolutely ensure that I have no contact with him. But on Father's Day this year, my son presented me with a card and on the envelope he had written, "I is never to late to be god." Along with this saying he had drawn a picture of our house, with flowers blooming outside, a rainbow in the sky, happy children playing, and someone in the sky wearing a hooded cloak. When I asked him what this all meant he explained to me that he would like me to become god so that I can end all war and bring peace to everyone, everywhere. I took him into my arms and, as gently as possible, thanked him and told him that such things are not gifts from the gods. We can only do what we all can, in our own small ways, as much as we are able, to work for peace, and that even daddies, even his own daddy who has never met a monster he has not vanquished or turned into a friend, even his daddy can only do a very little when it comes to such things.

20

It is the end of the school year. My son is done Grade Two, my daughter is done Kindergarten completely. As I carry home backpacks stuffed with workbooks and mementos, I ask them, "Out of everything you learned this year, what's the most important thing to remember?" Without hesitation, they both replied, "To be kind."

(A moment after, there is an odd noise in the air above us, some kind of bird noise but not like any I'd heard before, and, looking up, we see a cloud of Robin's feathers floating fifteen feet in the air above us. There are no trees, rooftops or wires nearby. There are no birds in sight. Just feathers, red, white, and black, drifting down.)

Second Intermission

WHERE MIGHT SHIPS FOUNDER: A POEM FOR MY SECOND OLDEST BROTHER ON THE OCCASION OF HIS BIRTHDAY

HE LISTENS MORE THAN he speaks and hears more than you say.

He knows that strength has limits and that the pain of the world is infinite and so, although he carries more than most, he does not carry more than he can bear. The ones he carries he carries well.

He knows that beauty, kindness, and love are infinite, too. And that a beer at the end of the day can help us remember this.

His eyes do a lot of his talking—"You're safe here" and "I honor your presence with me" and "I'm not going to touch your body with my hands or with my gaze" (a rare statement to find in the eyes of a man)—things that don't so much add to a conversation as make it possible in the first place. He makes it easy to speak in a way that feels honest.

He is gentle like a grizzly nursing her cubs. I'm pretty sure he is our mom's favorite (and, when I was younger, I had to get used to the fact that whenever I introduced him to my friends, they were going to like him more than they liked me).

He is my brother and my friend and I love him devotedly, ferociously, playfully, stupidly. He was always cooler than I, but never stopped finding ways to invite me to share life together with him. Shortly after my parents kicked me out, he invited me down to Windsor to spend the weekend visiting with him and his friends. They were all in University and I was still in high school. This made me feel special at a time when I generally felt like a piece of shit. Later, when he invited me to work at the camp where he worked, I felt the same way. When my heart was a raging ocean, he helped me find safe passage through the storm.

The Second Part: Father

And when his heart was a raging ocean he turned to the cliffs and carved himself a bay. His wife worked alongside of him and together they made a home for themselves. Their daughters are growing up beside those still waters. And although they are still young, their legs are taller than mountains and, one day, they will walk across the sea and storms that cause mighty ships to founder will only come up to their knees.

The Third Part

Fatherland

"It's like watching a murder mystery, only everyone is a murderer."[1]

---

1. My son, seven-and-one-half years old, after watching the last ten minutes of Leni Riefenstahl's *Triumph des Willens* (1935), with me.

1

IT IS IN THE Spring of 2017 when I begin to dream of the boy with puss in his eyes. He is young, 8 maybe 9 years old, and he is barefoot and shirtless, wearing a threadbare pair of pants, and he comes and stands at the foot of my bed. His hair is dark and cut short. He is Indigenous. I think Kanien'kehá:ka but maybe Anishinaabe. His eyes are so full of puss that he is blind. Thick, white and yellow discharge covers the entire periorbital region.

At that time, I was writing an independent research paper on the Mohawk Institute, Canada's oldest and longest running Indian Residential School, which was still standing an hour's drive from me. Survivors more frequently refer to the place as the Mush Hole (from very early on, children took a hymn they were taught—"There is a happy land far, far away/ Where Saints in glory stand bright, bright as day"—and changed it to "There is a boarding school far away/ Where we get mush'n'milk three times a day")[1]. I read through thousands of microfiches held in the National Archives in Ottawa, perusing financial statements, media clippings, letters to and from the school from various officials in the Department of Indian Affairs, student logs, and medical reports. Along the way, I also discovered the following note buried within the archive: "To enable this file to be made available to researchers it has been necessary for IAND officials to exclude some material in accordance with Cabinet Directive No. 46 of 7 June 1973."[2] I never did figure out what Cabinet Direct No. 46 of 7 June 1973 actually said. I go through online articles. I speak with a few survivors and others now associated with the project to restore the building so that it can stand as a testimony to what was done (it is, at this point, the only Indian Residential School left standing; all

---

1. See Graham, *The Mush Hole*, 382.
2. Library and Archives of Canada. School File Series—1879–1953 (RG 10-B-3-d), C-7935-00814.

others were torn down, allowed to rot into the earth and air and water, or significantly renovated and repurposed). Along the way, I read a report about a young boy, a student during the tenure of Reverend Canon C. J. Zimmerman, the Principal who was nicknamed "Skin" by the students because of the delight he took in publicly stripping students and placing them in sexually vulnerable positions prior to beating or whipping them, and this young boy was diagnosed with gonorrhea in his eyes.

For the first few nights the boy merely stands at the foot of my bed and observes me. Then, he moves up to the side of my bed, the side I was facing, and quietly begins to call to me. His arms hang loose at his sides. He never tries to touch me with anything but his voice. I don't know what words he is using, but I know that he is calling me. That night, the night he stood at the side of my bed for the first time, I continually wake up but he disappears when I do. The next night, when he came to call me, I decided to stay asleep but, this time, without warning, he yelled a yell that was also a scream, his mouth bursting open, the noise exploding out of him, and I woke up to the sound of my own voice yelling, my mouth burst open. I went back to sleep and I dreamed he was pulling at my bedding and throwing things out of my closet to try and wake me. When I awoke, all my pillows were on the floor and all the clothes I kept on shelves beside my bed had been pulled out onto the pillows.

The next day I smudged.

Later, while reading survivor testimonies in Elizabeth Graham's exceptional self-published book on the Mush Hole (no Canadian publisher was willing to print the information she collected), I came across a story told by an older girl who gained access to the boys' dormitories and discovered, there, a young boy whose eyes were full of puss. This is her account:

> I had a girlfriend and her brother—I don't know whatever happened to him—he was lying in bed—it seems like that's all he did all day, lying in bed, and there was white mucus coming out of his eyes. I don't think he was ever cared for medically. I've often wondered if he ended up blind, or what happened to him.[3]

I wonder if he is the same boy mentioned in the medical report—the boy with gonorrhea in his eyes. The same boy who visits me in my dreams. I wonder how a little boy, no older than my son, gets gonorrhea in his eyes and I think there is only one answer and I think it is not only the mush fed to the

---

3. Graham, The Mush Hole, 394.

The Third Part: Fatherland

students—often rotting, often crawling with maggots and other larvae, which the children were forced to eat again (frequently up to three times in a row) if they vomited it back up—that caused the children to gag.[4]

---

4. This information about how children were force-fed their own vomit, was shared with me in a conversation with Jessica Powless at the Mohawk Institute in December 2016. It was further affirmed and repeated to me in conversations I had at the Mohawk Institute with Amos Key Jr. and Virve Wiland in January and February of 2017.

2

THE TOWNSPEOPLE, THE SETTLERS, the white people, the Christians, complain about dirty, poorly clothed Indigenous children running away from the Institute to steal food from the garbage dump or from the swill they put out for their pigs. This was brought to the attention of the Department of Indian Affairs and so the Principal writes a reassuring letter that children were "punished thoroughly" for doing this.[1] The City responds by spraying chemicals on food disposed of in the dump to prevent children from eating there.[2] The townspeople much prefer to see the children scrubbed clean and singing carols at the Institute's annual Christmas pageant, a highly publicized and always successful local social, where the media praises the staff members and the Department of Indian Affairs for taking such sad and dirty savages ("coons" and "little niggers" as the articles call them) and transforming them into model Christian children.[3]

In 1913, when Principal A. Nelles nearly beat a runaway child to death in front of the townspeople, a few people objected but Nelles continued on in his job and, as far as I can tell from the redacted record that remains, no one at all complained about the Principals who sent teenage Indigenous

---

1. Complaints about kids eating from the garbage dump are originally treated dismissively by the Department of Indian Affairs but Principal Snell acknowledges that it does happen. However, he says that the boys who do this are punished "thoroughly" (Library and Archives of Canada. School File Series—1879–1953 (RG 10-B-3-d), C-7933-01250-51; also C-7933-01254). Several former students remember going to the dump for food (see Graham, *The Mush Hole*, 361, 363, 405).

2. Graham, *The Mush Hole*, 418–19.

3. See Library and Archives of Canada. School File Series—1879–1953 (RG 10-B-3-d), C-7933-00761. For a more detailed study of this, refer to Anderson and Robertson, *Seeing Red*.

girls to local parties as escorts intended to entertain the men. And by "entertain" I mean "be forced to have sex with."[4]

There are whispered rumors that these girls also underwent forced sterilizations to prevent pregnancies taking place, although there is no hard evidence of such (by "hard evidence" I mean "things that a Eurocentric, post-Enlightenment scientific model of knowledge/power accept as evidence"). Forced sterilizations of Indigenous peoples, however, was practiced elsewhere by the Canadian Government and the Canadian Medical establishment, up into the 1970s (after which, abortion was legalized and doctors were able to abort Indigenous children, regardless of the wishes of the mother, if the doctors determined that an abortion was in the best interest of the family—thus, for example, a doctor could determine a family was too poor to have another child and terminate the pregnancy regardless of what the woman wanted or even understood about what was happening).[5]

---

4. This information was shared with me by Jessica Powless at the Mohawk Institute in December 2016. See also the "Mohawk Institute Indian Residential School IAP School Narrative" posted online by the National Centre for Truth and Reconciliation; available here: http://nctr.ca/School%20narratives/EAST/ON/MOHAWK%20INSTITUTE.pdf.

5. On these forced sterilizations, refer to Stote, *An Act of Genocide*.

3

I TWICE WENT TO visit the Mohawk Institute. The first time I participated in a guided tour of the building and grounds. The second time I met with the archivist and a prominent elder. There is salt around the windows and around the edges of the dormitory rooms. Medicine bundles hang over many doorways and windows. Entry to much of the basement is not permitted. Many of the sexual assaults took place there, with the muffled screams of children (the youngest on record being barely 3 years old) overwhelmed by the noise of machinery—the boiler, the laundry machines, the pipes, constantly in need of repair, everything constantly in need of repair, and when work became absolutely essential to prevent the place from collapsing totally, contracts were consistently awarded to the lowest bidder, leading to the same repairs being needed again within a year—clanking and hissing and moaning and dripping.

(The muffled screams of children being raped by the men and sometimes women who were supposed to be caring for them . . . in what kind of world is this even thinkable, let alone possible, let alone ubiquitous, let alone brushed aside by Canadians and their Government who say, in so many ways, that's in the past now, shouldn't they be over it?)

The archivist says that some nights the spirit of a man emerges from the boiler room and tries to gain entry to the rooms that used to be the dormitories. She says he is looking for children. She says he is an evil spirit. She says he goes first to the rooms were the youngest children stayed.

The children burned the school down on multiple occasions. This happened first in 1859. Then in 1905, Isaiah Antone, Roy Wilson, Jesse Debo, and Frank Winnie burned down the school building in April, the barns in May, and an external play house for boys in June.[1] It is likely that these

---

[1]. Information about the fires was shared with me by Jessica Powless at the Mohawk Institute in December 2016. It was further affirmed and repeated to me in further

The Third Part: Fatherland

boys were either sentence to hard labor in Kingston Penitentiary (where children were imprisoned alongside of grown men) or sent to Reformatory Schools that the children appear to have feared even more than the Residential Schools. In 1955, the barns were burned again, killing much of the livestock and destroying all of the feed. But, every time, the school was rebuilt. This was the will of the Great White Father.

In fact, the Canadian Government was always keen to be more involved in running the Mush Hole. Several times, it attempted to wrest control from the New England Company, an evangelical British Missionary Society, which worked closely with the Anglican Diocese of Huron in staffing and managing the school (the federal Government was, primarily, the funding body).[2] The Government attempted a coup after Principal H. W. Snell was forced into retirement at the age of 65 due to ongoing concerns about how he handled the Institute's finances (Snell, in turn, had replaced Principal Rogers due to his public drunkenness and the way he used Indigenous children as slave labor on his own farm; this well illustrates the priorities of both the Government and the Anglicans—spending as little money as possible, studiously avoiding any public scandal, and killing the Indian in the child). The Department of Indian Affairs attempted to install a Christian Indigenous man from the local Six Nations Reserve as the Principal. The Anglicans were appalled and a concerted, State-wide media and letter writing campaign was undertaken. On November 6, 1944, the Most Reverend P. Carrington, Archbishop of Québec and Metropolitan of the Anglican Church of Canada, a man who, early on in his career had done considerable work with the Boy Scouts, launched the Campaign with a letter to the Department's Secretary. He wrote:

> I am informed that the Department is considering the idea of radically changing the whole character of the School by putting it under a Layman as a Principal and merely allowing the services of a Chaplain for our own children.
>
> I was very much shocked when I heard of this proposal to bring to an end a religious and educational tradition which has

---

conversations I had at the Mohawk Institute with Amos Key Jr. and Virve Wiland in January and February of 2017. Further information is also available in Library and Archives of Canada. School File Series—1879–1953 (RG 10-B-3-d), C-7933-01189; and in the "Mohawk Institute Indian Residential School IAP School Narrative" posted online by the National Centre for Truth and Reconciliation; available here: http://nctr.ca/School%20narratives/EAST/ON/MOHAWK%20INSTITUTE.pdf.

2. On this feud, see especially, Graham, *The Mush Hole*, 165–209.

A Magnificent Work

been established for so long, and I am sure that Anglicans generally throughout Canada would hear of this decision with regret and amazement.[3]

Immediately after Archbishop Carrington posted his letter, letters arrived at the Department of Indian Affairs from Anglican Bishops all across Canadian occupied territories. The Bishop of the Arctic (where Indigenous men and women were being sent to southern Indian Hospitals, often hijacked with no notice given, to be forcibly sterilized or treated for other ailments and, when symptoms persisted, many languished for years, dying without ever seeing their families again) writes:

> May I point out that no one who has any intimate knowledge of our native people could fail to realize that it is of first rate importance that the children shall not only be taught those things which are important so that they may have such knowledge as will fit them for the life they will be called upon to live but also they should be trained in a religious atmosphere. This is necessary in order that they may have that moral stamina without which they would go down in defeat . . . more help and not less should be given for their spiritual upbringing.[4]

The Bishop of Ottawa says more or less the same thing.[5] The Bishops of Athabasca and New Westminster both emphasize the remarkably good work Anglicans are already doing at the Mohawk Institute, and the Bishop of Niagara along with the Bishop of Brandon emphasizes what a loss this change would be to the Indian children who attend the school.[6] The Bishop of Caledonia waxes eloquent along these lines: "let a magnificent work alone and allow it not only to carry on in the same successful way as in the past but give it the opportunity to still further develop its beneficent policies for our natives in that Reserve."[7] The Bishop of Ontario is

3. Library and Archives of Canada. School File Series—1879–1953 (RG 10-B-3-d), C-7934-01464.

4 Library and Archives of Canada. School File Series—1879–1953 (RG 10-B-3-d), C-7933-01467 and C-7933-01468

5. Library and Archives of Canada. School File Series—1879–1953 (RG 10-B-3-d), C-7933-01470.

6. See, in the order that they are mentioned above, Library and Archives of Canada. School File Series—1879–1953 (RG 10-B-3-d), C-7933-1476; C-7933-1483; C-7933-1484; C-7933-01487.

7. Library and Archives of Canada. School File Series—1879–1953 (RG 10-B-3-d), C-7933-01495.

The Third Part: Fatherland

not far behind him.[8] Other Bishops, make the veiled threat in Archbishop Carrington's letter more explicit. The Bishop of Keewatin warns that any change would "stir serious misgivings among the members of the Church of England in Canada" and the Bishop of Edmonton suggests the same.[9] The Bishop of British Columbia is the most threatening of all using words like "aggressive" and "militant" when speaking of how Anglicans will react if the proposed changes are made.[10]

In the end, the Government does let the magnificent work alone and, with glowing recommendations from all parties, the Anglicans appoint Reverend Canon C. J. Zimmerman as the new Principal.[11] He remains Principal for the next twenty-five years, until the school closes in 1970. After the closure (when he and his wife, Gladys, who was hospitalized for depression multiple times, sometimes for weeks at a time, destroyed several boxes of records), he continued to serve as the chaplain of the Her Majesty's Royal Chapel of the Mohawks. They lived rent free on the grounds of the school until their deaths (his in '82, hers in '84). In his obituary, it is noted that, due to his service at the Mohawk Institute, he was made an honorary member of the Six Nations and given the Mohawk Name "De has swa" which, in English, means "The Enlightener."[12] The obituary doesn't mention that Indigenous children had already given him the name "Skin" (it does mention that some of his descendants live in the same city as me, but I was unable to find them—in fact, in my research I was unable to track down any former staff members or their families).[13]

---

8. Library and Archives of Canada. School File Series—1879–1953 (RG 10-B-3-d), C-7933-01497.

9. Library and Archives of Canada. School File Series—1879–1953 (RG 10-B-3-d), Respectively, C-7933-01472; C-7933-01491.

10. Library and Archives of Canada. School File Series—1879–1953 (RG 10-B-3-d), C-7933-01489.

11. For the details of the wrangling back and forth between Indian Affairs and the Anglican Church of Canada, see the following letters that are on file: Library and Archives of Canada. School File Series—1879–1953 (RG 10-B-3-d), C-7933-01515; C-7933-015-16, 44–46, 50–54, 56, 58–59, 77–79; C-7933-0615-17, 33–35, 49, 80; C-7934-00179; my perspective here is also informed by my correspondence with Paula Whitlow in September 2016, and by my conversation with Virve Wiland, and Amos Key Jr. in January 2017.

12. This obituary is available online here: boards.ancestry.com/localities.northam.canada.ontario.brant/7824/mb.ashx.

13. On Zimmerman being given the name "Skin," see, Graham, The Mush Hole, 396–97, 399–401, 404, 409, 411–12, 422. Jessica Powless also spoke about Zimmerman in this way in my conversation with her in December 2016, as did Virve Wilson and

A Magnificent Work

It is impossible to know how many children Skin tortured and raped while he was Principal. It is known that he sometimes raped children in the Chapel, other times in his office. Once, a boy he stripped and tied to a picnic table and then whipped, screamed so loud that the surrounding farms heard the cries.[14] Eventually the screaming ended, a tortured child can only scream for so long, but a man can whip that child for much longer. And that's what happened.

(Whipping a child so that his screams carry across the miles, until he can scream no more, and continuing to whip that child even though he can no longer scream . . . in what kind of world is this even thinkable, let alone possible, let alone ubiquitous, let alone brushed aside by Canadians and their Government who say, in so many ways, that's in the past now, shouldn't they be over it?)

When it comes to Christianity, colonialism, and Canadian paternalism, enshrined also in the Indian Act of 1867, wherein Canada adopts the posture of a Father caring for "our Indigenous peoples" who are, universally, regardless of age, portrayed as children (in need of both instruction and discipline), this certainly is enlightening.

Amos Key Jr., in my conversations with them in January and February, 2017.

14. Mentioned in conversation with Virve Wiland and Amos Key Jr. Also mentioned in Graham, *The Mush Hole*, 420; and it is worth also referring to the following news article: Ashley Csanady, "'Where I learned to fight and cheat and steal': Six Nations wants to save longest running residential school," *National Post*; available online: news/nationalpost.com/news/Canada/where-i-learned-to-fight-and-cheat-and-steal-six-nations-wants-to-save-longest-running-residential-school. Other examples of Zimmerman's cruelty are abundant in survivor stories—from force feeding a girl until she vomited, to causing permanent kidney damage in another girl by kicking her in the back, to leaving scars on a boy's back because he (Zimmerman) exhausted himself beating the boy to try and make him cry, to putting tacks into the strap, to beating a boy so badly that he caused permanent brain damage, to stripping a couple naked and beating them in front of one another and the staff members, to lashing children with an extension cord (Graham, *The Mush Hole*, 391, 401–2, 404, 418, 424). Zimmerman was said to act nice when other people were around but cruelly when there was no witness (Graham, *The Mush Hole*, 396). Some survivors describe him as a sadist (Graham, *The Mush Hole*, 402).

4

THE CHILDREN AT THE Mohawk Institute were not permitted to have names. Instead, upon intake, they were given a uniform, their heads were shaved and a chemical delousing powder was applied to their scalps (the powder burned their scalps and often prevented them from sleeping the first night), any possessions were confiscated and each kid was assigned a number.[1] Under the sewing tables, scratched into the wood, one finds what appear to be mathematical equations ("22 + 51" and so on) but these are, in fact, the equivalent of the "Johnny + Sarah" that we find in on the walls of public-school bathroom stalls.[2] Because they were allowed no possessions, things like gum wrappers and bottle caps, detritus, became treasures and stashes were found inside walls and crawl spaces throughout the school. Some survivors recall one little girl who cuddled with a broken piece of glass every night because it was the only thing she owned.

I saw some of these stashes of what anyone else would consider garbage when I visited the Institute, and I thought a lot about how my daughter, too, collects gravel, random pieces of paper she finds on the playground, and beach glass. But, at night, she cuddles with me in a room full of books and toys and games, and, in the dark, one of her names is Beloved.

---

1. Shared with me in conversation with Jessica Powless in December, 2016, and in conversations with Vivre Wiland and Amos Key Jr. in January and February, 2017. It is a profoundly disturbing experience to visit the Mohawk Institute now and see this delousing, identity-erasing room and the bathrooms next to it where multiple child-sized bathtubs were installed in rows. I recently described this experience to a Polish friend and she responded by saying that, "this sounds like what I saw at Auschwitz."

2. Photos of this graffiti are available online. See Donna Kell (photos by Donna Kell and Jodi Bar), "Mohawk Institute Residential School: A Life-Changing Visit for IAP2 Practitioners," IAP2 Canada Blog, December 13, 2016; https://iap2canada.wordpress.com/2016/12/13/mohawk-institute-residential-school-a-life-changing-visit-for-iap2-practitioners/

5

LORNA (AT THE MUSH Hole from 1940–945), as told to Elizabeth Graham:

> I think the real terrible thing that happened to me—I'm trying to figure out what was the most terrible thing other than just being there without a family . . . There was a lot of feeling of abandonment—aloneness. Aloneness every day. That feeling of not having anybody, of being so lonesome. We knew our Dad and we knew our sister, and we knew what it was like to be with them, and how we felt, and the difference of being there with nobody was really traumatic . . . My sister was there too with me when I was there. To hear her lonesome cries—my goodness!—it would have been better if I was there by myself. She was my father's baby. She had turned five when she went. To hear her cry and hear her holler "Daddy," was worse than my lonesomeness. I used to put my arms around her and say "Don't cry, don't cry," and I'd be crying. Then we'd both be crying. She was very much a baby.[1]

Lorna's sister was 4½ when she was first taken to the school. My son was 4½ when he stood on the window ledge in my bedroom and cried, "I've lost my mommy!" and it was the saddest cry I'd ever heard. But my son came around just fine. He's a silly, gentle, smart, and happy boy. But I think about those dorms full of shattered children—I think about Lorna's sister and about the boys' dorm which always smelled of pee (some said it was because the boys were so scared and homesick, some said it was because they were "sodomized" by the staff members but, whatever the cause, and it was almost certainly a combination of both, the staff members treated bedwetters by rubbing their faces in their own urine and sometimes excrement, and giving them electric shock therapy, and the staff members persisted in doing this, although neither form of therapy proved effective)—and I think,

---

1. Graham, *The Mush Hole*, 375, 377.

my god, what have we done?² And tonight I spent a little extra time rubbing my daughter's back as she fell asleep and I told her I loved her one or two times more than usual and I gave her some extra kisses on her cheeks which have never known violence, and then I tickled my son's arm and played with his hair, and tickled that back of his neck which made him sigh his happy sighs, and I said, "Have a good sleep," and he smiled at me awhile and then he said, "You, too." And then I came to write but I needed to stop and cry a little while first. Because Lorna's sister. She was #63. And she cried for her daddy ("I've lost my mommy!") and he never came. And I think Lorna and her sister, #63, are still crying, and I am, too, and I don't know how to get over this and what does that even mean?

---

2. Regarding responses to bed-wetting, a personal friend shared their experiences of this with me in 2013. It is also discussed in Graham, *The Mush Hole*, 366, 376, 378.

6

WHEN SURVIVORS OF THE school began to gather in the '90s, it is said that, for the first five years, nobody spoke of what they had experienced. Instead, people cried together. They cried together and held each other.

After the lawsuits start, the New England Company which still operates and, to this day, refuses to apologize or take any responsibility and, in their self-published history of their missionary work, expresses resentment that misguided legal cases have resulted in "the siphoning off of very large amounts of money from charitable endeavors, which could have benefited the needy in the native community."[1] Instead, the Company blames the Indigenous peoples and the Government of Canada. The Canadian Government, in turn, finally issued a formal apology for residential schools via Prime Minister Stephen Harper in 2008 (a transcription of it now hangs in the front entrance of the Mohawk Institute).[2] Then, in 2009, Harper stated that Canada has no history of colonialism and proceeded to try and enact legislation that would altogether, once and for all, terminate Indigenous identity, treaty rights, and any Indigenous claims to sovereignty in Canadian-occupied territories.[3] As for the Anglican Church, it, too, apologized (after a consultation with its legal team to ensure that nothing said in the lawsuit could be used against the Church in Court), but if you go now to their official website about the Mohawk Institute, you find no mention of the rampant physical, sexual, emotional, and psychological abuse of the

---

1. See Hitchin and the Governor and Court of the New England Company, *'Come Over and Help Us,'* 45.

2. For this apology see, *Statement of apology to former students of Indian Residential Schools*; available online here: ://www.aadnc-aandc.gc.ca/eng/1100100015644/1100100015649

3. Regarding Harper's comments to the G20, see David Ljunggren, "Every G20 nation wants to be Canada, insists PM," available online here: http://www.reuters.com/article/columns-us-g20-canada-advantages-idUSTRE58P05Z20090926

children who were forced to attend.[4] The children tried to escape this. They ran away, but were regularly hunted down, dragged out of their homes, and taken back to the school by RCMP officers.[5] One runaway, Joseph Commanda, who was thirteen years old when he died in 1959, was killed when he was struck by a train trying to elude capture by the Police.[6] RCMP Officers were also dispatched to take children—often at gunpoint—from families who refused to send them. Runaways returned to the Institute were, at times, dressed as convicts with shaved heads, but after some complaints about this, were more frequently, locked in a blacked out closet used as a solitary confinement punishment cell where they were left, often for days, with little or nothing to eat or drink (Blanche Hill-Easton describes how the vertebrae in her neck became fused because of the way in which she was slammed into that closet; this is a long-term painful condition, all the more painful as one first experiences it, as a child, alone, on the floor of a dark closet).[7] Others were forced to "run the gauntlet," and crawl between the legs of 50–70 of their peers, while being struck by anything at hand (and the striking was often very hard because the other students were deprived of privileges if any student ran away).[8] Any Indigenous people living on Reserves who were found to be "harboring fugitives" were prosecuted as criminals and fined or condemned to prison (sometimes the government tried to scare people off of this by charging those who harbored fugitives with rape).[9] Consequently, in a terse and guarded statement, the Commissioner

---

4. See Anglican Church of Canada, "A message from Primate, Archbishop Michael Peters, to the National Native Convocation, Minaki, Ontario, Friday, August 6, 1993" in *Truth and Reconciliation*; available online here: http://www.anglican.ca/tr/apology/english. In terms of what they have on their official website, see here: http://www.anglican.ca/tr/histories/mohawk-institute/.

5. For sample RCMP reports on bringing back truants, see Library and Archives of Canada. School File Series—1879–1953 (RG 10-B-3-d), C-7933-00843; C-7933-00391, although many more reports like these exist on the record.

6. See Milloy, *A National Crime*, 286.

7. See Graham, *The Mush Hole*, 9, 23, 384, 388–89, 414; also Library and Archives of Canada. School File Series—1879–1953 (RG 10-B-3-d), C-7933-00912; even the government recognized that large numbers of runaways strongly suggested that something might be very wrong at the Mohawk Institute (see C-7933-00788). For Blanche Hill-Easton's account, see here Gamble, "Tales of the Mush Hole retold," *Brantford Expositor*; available online here: www.brantfordexpositor.ca/2012/08/24/tales-of-the-mush-hole-retold.

8. Graham, *The Mush Hole*, 387, 391.

9. See Library and Archives of Canada. School File Series—1879–1953 (RG 10-B-3-d), C-7935-00395; C-7935-00420; and C-7935-00422.

of the RCMP also apologized a few years ago.[10] But the RCMP is also now under investigation for the role it has played in the disappearance and murder of Indigenous women across these territories.

(And Cindy Gladue, too, had her torso removed so that her lacerated vagina, with a fatal 11-centimetre wound, could be taken into Court as evidence in a trial where the white man who raped and killed her was found innocent by a mostly white jury, and this torso now sits as State's evidence in a refrigerated locker awaiting the day when it will again be pulled out and poked and prodded and magnified on a display screen, in an appeal that is set to take place, in no small part, because a public outcry has driven the Crown to continue to pursue a case that it would otherwise have preferred to have forgotten.)

The words of Blanche still ring in my ears: "We're never going to heal ... We're like a faceless people on this land."[11]

---

10. See, Royal Canadian Mounted Police, "RCMP Apology," available online here: http://www.rcmp-grc.gc.ca/aboriginal-autochtone/apo-reg-eng.htm.

11. As quoted by Richard Beales, "We're never going to heal," *Brantford Expositor*; available online here: www.brantfordexpositor.ca/2008/12/15/were-never-going-to-heal.

7

MEMO FROM LOCAL DISTRICT Superintendent Randle.

> New arrivals: Gary Ronald Hill, Marion Rebecca Hill, Carolyn Ann Jacobs, Lorne Gibson, Milford Gibson, Barbara Louise Hill, Pauline Joan Henry.
> Discharges: No. 1296, 1309, 1313, 01307, 10317, 10334, 01342, 01360, 01185, 01224, 012363, 01272, 01275, 01341, 01343, 01284.[1]

We can guess what happened to the new arrivals. It is harder to know what happened to the discharges and under what circumstances they were discharged. We do know that approximately fifty percent of the students who attended the school died of malnutrition, infectious diseases, trauma, and violence, and we also now know that the school often discharged children (back to family or to the local Indian Hospital, which employed unlicensed physicians, engaged in experimental medical practices on its patients, and was not staffed adequately to maintain any sort of hygienic environment) shortly before they died in order to keep the number of reported deaths as low as possible.[2]

Hence, digging through the archives, I discovered the story of Reuben Fox, a boy discharged to the hospital due to a mastoid infection. Reuben

---

1. Library and Archives of Canada. School File Series—1879–1953 (RG 10-B-3-d), C-7935-00791.

2. On the uses of "Indian Hospitals" in Canadian-occupied territories, see Lux, *Separate Beds*. Multiple reports demonstrate officials trying to discharge dying children from schools in order to keep their death rates lower; see, for example, Library and Archives of Canada. School File Series—1879–1953 (RG 10-B-3-d), C-7935-00895–96 and C-7933-00819. This makes lists of discharges look particularly ominous (as, for example, file #C-7935-00607 mentions 23 discharges at the beginning of November, 1949, but where the students are discharged to, or what kind of state they are in, is not mentioned).

A Magnificent Work

was listless, lacked all energy, and was not expected to recover.[3] At last, his father was called to the hospital in order to say goodbye but—to the surprise of the doctors and nurses—Reuben then recovered in a remarkable way and his mood completely altered from one of hopelessness to one of joy (as one report states, "So much did the boy improve that the Doctor thought a complete recovery would result"). But then Reuben contracted Tubercular Meningitis—frequently endemic at the Institute and the Hospital—and died.

This story of a son, literally dying because he was forcibly taken from his family, because the Canadian State considered itself and its surrogates a better father than the dad who gave him life and who wanted to stay with him always, who then recovers when his dad comes for him, but who ultimately dies because, at the end of the day, this is about genocide and my fatherland, my home and native land, is incredibly efficient at genocide, is emblematic of all of this. I imagine the grief of the father, rushing to see his son one more time before he dies, I imagine the delight and gratitude when Reuben recovers, I imagine the world-destroying grief when his son dies. And I imagine Reuben and the way he must have felt, and I remember my son crawling into bed with me with tears in his eyes asking, "Am I going to die?" and I remember my daughter wailing, "I don't want to die! I don't want to die!" and Reuben died and his father, somehow (but how?) returned home from the hospital. Some hospitals use disguised linen carts to move dead children from their beds to the morgue so as not to upset any passersby, but Reuben's father also disappears just as quietly and inoffensively from the record. Here was a father's love strong enough to bring his son back from the brink of death, but we killed them anyway. Both of them.

And that's the end of the story of Reuben Fox. It is a very small story. No bigger than 11-centimetres.

---

3. See Library and Archives of Canada. School File Series—1879–1953 (RG 10-B-3-d), C-7935-00857-58.

8

Unanswered letter, February 10, 1949.

"I want release for my daughter Mildred Horne, she is at Mohawk Institute, she is restless at school and seems to lost interest there I have a good place over here for her."[1]

---

1. See Library and Archives of Canada. School File Series—1879–1953 (RG 10-B-3-d), C-7935-00407.

9

I.

WHEN OUR CAR CAME abreast of the trees lining the front of the property, I was hit with a sudden and overwhelming wave of grief. I only just stopped myself from yelling in surprise and pain. The trees, I realized, the trees remember. They witnessed it all, over the last two hundred years (very early pictures show them as saplings freshly planted on the grounds of the Institute), they heard the cries of the children, they saw their emaciated bodies, they witnessed the death of Effie Smith when a one hundred pound wheel from a neglected, makeshift swing feel on her chest and crushed her (the subsequent investigation found that no one was at fault for this . . . or for anything . . . ever).[1] The trees witnessed the families approaching the front steps and parents departing alone. At night, they saw the seven and eight year old children, children no bigger than my son and daughter, climb out of windows and scale down the sheer brick walls from the upper floors where their dorms were located, in order to try and sneak food back from the orchard to feed themselves, their friends, and the little ones in the dorms below them. And they heard, the next day, how the children cried out when lined up for their morning inspection and beating (it is said that those who were being sexually abused by staff members were beaten especially brutally in order to try and ensure that they remained silent). The trees were witnesses of generation, after generation, after generation, with children eventually coming from as far away as the Northwest Territories and Québec as the Anglicans worked increasingly hard to keep the facility open, while also trying to prevent truancies and runaways. By then,

---

1. On Effie Smith see Library and Archives of Canada. School File Series—1879–1953 (RG 10-B-3-d), C-7935-01399–01420 (and note how the record moves from one of anxiety about consequences to self-exoneration on behalf of all the officials involved). This even is also remembered by some survivors interviewed in Graham, *The Mush Hole*, 370.

however, the closure of the Institute was a foregone conclusion. The federal Government had shifted its strategy to social services and began to steal Indigenous children from their communities (still with the assistance of the RCMP) and adopt them out into white families, cutting off all contact with their families of origin, in what became known as "the '60s scoop" (the first wave of this took place in the 1960s, although the practice continues today and, at present, there are more Indigenous children in foster care in Canadian-occupied territories than were ever in attendance in the Indian Residential Schools).[2] The trees saw, felt, heard, and lived through it all.

And after touring the building and walking out into the night air, rattled and gasping and suppressing white tears, I walked down a small hill, through the grass already dewy, and I rested my head for a good long time against one of those trees. I felt its quiet strength and I lifted my hands in gratitude.

"Trees are god reaching up from the earth to hug us" and the blood that cried out from the soil still cried out, and we got into our car and went home to our families.

I heard that cry once before, in 2014, when I heard Tanya Tagaq sing for the first time. But to speak about that, I need to say a little more about trees.

II.

When I was in my early twenties, I spent a few summers working for a small tree planting company. Tree planting companies are subcontractors of the lumber mills and the massive Canadian logging industry. Tree planters do not restore the environment—the land, the rivers, the mountains, the plants, and the animals will not be the same and no effort is made to actually return things to the state they were in before everything got torn up and turned into money. Rather, the intention is to simply pack as much future lumber into the land as can fit according to the latest satellite GPS mapping technology. It's not so much an investment in the future of the planet as an investment in the future profits of the mills (the Government made reforestation a requirement for logging companies sometime in the '70s, I believe, although even when I was planting trees in the early 2000s, we would still sometimes plant giant clear cuts from the '70s). So even though logging companies will tell you that there are more trees in the ground here today than seventy years ago, and that growth exceeds removal, this is because more lumber is being packed into the land (which

---

2. On the Sixties Scoop, see Crey and Fournier, *Stolen From Our Embrace*.

A Magnificent Work

is then bombed with pesticides to prevent other plants from growing in order to ensure that the desired kind of lumber survives—i.e. if you are trying to cultivate spruce or pine seedlings, you don't want alders taking over everything and choking them out, so you create a pesticide that kills alders and other plants [and animals] but leaves the spruce and pine untouched). So, sure, more trees. More seedlings than old growth forests. And entire ecosystems are being destroyed and turned into private woodlots (a very Heideggerian standing-reserve).

III.

As a planter, I spent some time working on unceded Wet'suwet'en territory, although I didn't know that at the time. I thought I was in northern British Columbia and, when I got back to Toronto from the summers I spent there, I always used to refer to my time planting as the "quintessential Canadian wilderness experience."

I am ashamed to think of that now—there is so much of the settler colonial ideology caught up in those few words (the implication of terra nullius, the total lack of awareness that the territory was never ceded to Canada, my ignorance of the caretakers of the land on which I walked . . .)—but those were the words I spoke and I am responsible for them.

IV.

Today, the Unist'ot'en Camp and the land defenders there who are working to prevent the tar sands pipeline from moving through their territories, along with folks like the Wilp Luutkudziiwus of the Gitxsan Nation at the Madii Lii Camp, and the Klabona Keepers, composed of Tahltan elders and families, are some of the people I find the most inspiring in the world. These are people who care deeply about the land and who act to prevent the land and water and air and plants and animals and people from being poisoned and torn apart and plundered and left for dead. The land—composed of all these entities, including the people—is calling out and these are the people who have heard that call and responded. It saddens me that I drank from streams in those territories and smelled the earth there after the rain, and watched the sunset over those mountains, and never once thought of these keepers of the land.

The Third Part: Fatherland

V.

As the summer winds down and tree-planting contracts come to an end, there is always the opportunity to make a fair bit of extra money by hopping from company to company as some contractors are increasingly desperate to get their trees in the ground before the end of August. A good many planters leave from August first onwards because they want to go and party and spend their money and travel before returning to school in September. I liked to stay at late as possible and so I would pack up my tent and my gear, find out where a camp was located and hitchhike down Highway 16 to the next job.

Highway 16 is known as the Highway of Tears. Indigenous groups report that over thirty indigenous women and girls have gone missing or been found dead along that stretch of highway, although official police estimates are much lower and sit at eighteen, with a slightly broader radius (officially and unofficially, the police and the Government of Canada have taken a stand of not wanting to do much about addressing the extraordinarily high rates at which Indigenous women go missing and being murdered in Canada).[3] At the time, I didn't know that I was hitchhiking on the Highway of Tears and, as an able-bodied (in peak physical condition), white, hetero, cis, male settler, I didn't experience any problems above and beyond the occasional nonsense a fellow like me can experience hitchhiking anywhere else on Turtle Island. I came home and told my friends that, really, hitchhiking is much safer than you would think. This is another thing for which I must take responsibility.

As I have reflected back on this experience over the years, it has come to represent to me a particularly vivid snapshot of the privilege I experience simply by being born as a certain kind of person at a certain time in history. Of course, this privilege isn't something I only experience when hitchhiking. I spent a number of years living just fine in Vancouver's downtown eastside where seventy mostly Indigenous women have gone missing. Partial remains of a number of those women were found at the Pickton pig farm, where they had been murdered, butchered and fed to pigs (the police had received a number of tips about investigating the Pickton farm but they never got around to doing much of anything about these missing women until there was finally enough public pressure for

---

3. Regarding the Highway of Tears, see McDiarmid, *Highway of Tears*.

them to engage in a more serious investigation).[4] This is one particularly striking example of a broader settler colonial phenomenon, where ongoing calls for an inquest into the murdered and missing Indigenous women in Canada eventually resulted in the Royal Canadian Mounted Police revealing that approximately twelve hundred Indigenous women are officially known to have gone missing or been murdered in these colonized territories since 1980 (the RCMP tried to lay most of the blame for this on Indigenous men and communities but public pressure has led to the federal Government orchestrating an inquiry into this although it appears that this Inquiry will be a total and very deliberate disaster). Estimates from grassroots organizations place the number of missing and murdered women much higher. These are women like Tina Fontaine, a fifteen-year-old girl, found in a weighted duvet in the Red River in Winnipeg. Women like Dawn Crey, whose DNA was found in the dirt of the Pickton farm. Women like Loretta Saunders, a University student who was engaged in a research project about murdered and missing Indigenous women, who disappeared and whose body was later found on a median beside a highway in New Brunswick. Despite all these things, Stephen Harper was quick to assert that all of this is a "criminal" matter and not a "sociological phenomenon". That, of course, is how Prime Ministers and the heads of Settler States—form Canada to Rhodesia—are wont to speak.

But there is a call rising up here as well—just like the land is calling—there is a call rising up from and with the Indigenous Peoples of these territories, and it is especially the women who are hearing and responding to (and making) this call.

This is the call I heard when listening to Tanya Tagaq. It was as though the land was singing, as though the blood of the missing and murdered Indigenous women, which has mixed with the earth and water and air, was crying out. And the cry was so strong that there were times when I was sitting with my stomach muscles flexed and I couldn't relax them because I felt like I was being punched in the stomach by the song. I wept and I listened to the voice of the Kuupak river delta—one of the largest in the world—singing its death song. I listened to the flocks of birds who died landing in the tailings ponds by Fort McMoney because they thought they

---

4. For the final report of this investigation see The National Inquiry into Missing and Murdered Indigenous Women and Girls, *Reclaiming Power and Place: The Final Report of the National Inquiry into Missing and Murdered Indigenous Women and Girls*; available online here: https://www.mmiwg-ffada.ca/final-report/. See also, Anderson, Campbell and Belcourt (eds)., *Keetsahnak / Our Missing and Murdered Indigenous Sisters*.

The Third Part: Fatherland

were bodies of water. I wept and I listened to the farewell song of the fish and the water and the plants and the animals and all the creeping things who died when Imperial Metals spilled 2.5 billion gallons of contaminated water and 4.5 million cubic meters of metals laden silt into Hazeltine Creek, Polley Lake and Quesnel Lake on the way to the Ltha Koh/Stolo/sat'atqwa7 River Watershed. And I listened to Tina. And I listened to Dawn. And I listened to Loretta. And I listened to the voices of a great cloud of witnesses crying out and bearing witness. I listened to the cry of blood and land and water and women. I listened to the voice of stolen life singing. Mountains have been turned into valleys. Rivers have been dammed. Marshes have been turned into toxic wastelands. Forests have been turned into woodlots.

And Indigenous women have been turned into meat.

But life that has been stolen cries out. I heard it in Tanya's song. And I heard it again at the Mohawk Institute.

10

To amuse themselves, and to make some money from townspeople who were keen to spectate and place bets, children were forced to box in makeshift rings in the playrooms.[1] Some survivors recall one boy forced to fight for fourteen hours straight in an elimination tournament. He broke his hands knocking out boy after boy until he was overwhelmed by exhaustion. Others remember one staff member offering boxing lessons to the boys in his office, only to relentlessly beat them, one by one, until the walls and floor were running with blood and pulp and gore. One of the Principals sometimes got into the ring with the boys. This litany of horrors was part of the curriculum deemed necessary to transform children into men.

Harrison Burning, as told to Elizabeth Graham:

> When I first went there, I cried and I cried and I cried and I cried, but it didn't help any. That's what they say about the kids—one day you're a boy, the next day you're a man—look after yourself...
>
> I believe it when people say they didn't learn to love in there. Like me—I often say "I have no heart"—I have no heart.[2]

These boys who became men, if they didn't die, if they were in the fifty percent who survived, sometimes went on to become fathers like the Reverend Principals and teachers and their Father in heaven. And so we find ourselves, twenty years after the closure of the Residential Schools, and many children in Indigenous communities are exhibiting the same symptoms of trauma as those exhibited by the students (suicide rates among Indigenous youth are some of the highest in the world and, if we narrow that down to Inuit youth, they are the highest in the world). Trauma passes

---

1. See Graham, *The Mush Hole*, 259, 360, 419. Jessica Powless also spoke about this in conversation with me in December 2016, as did Virve Wiland and Amos Key Jr., in January and February, 2017.

2. Graham, *The Mush Hole*, 357.

The Third Part: Fatherland

from generation to generation. And Canada encourages this and offers it as proof of the savagery and immaturity of "our Indigenous peoples" who are dying because they have not assimilated well. Although assimilation, as Canada has pursued it, qualifies for the UN definition of genocide, so instead of assimilation Canada now talks about reconciliation. But it means the same thing.

Quando all patria si e' dato tutto, non si e' ancora dato abbastanza. (That is to say, "when everything is given to the fatherland, it is still not enough"—a frequent refrain of Italian soldiers during the Second World War.)

11

AFTER MY RESEARCH HAD ended, I had a dream about a very tall, very proper, and very stern-looking fifty-year-old man who was tasked with maintaining the buildings and grounds of a very old estate. He spends his days doing upkeep, maintenance and repairs on the labyrinthine Edwardian manor house, the lawns, the barns where dairy cattle had been housed, the chicken coops, the orchard, the greenhouse, and the fields but, no matter how hard he works, he cannot keep up with the rate at which everything is decaying. No sooner does he fix one leak in the roof than another appears. No sooner does he fix a sagging section of flooring, than a pipe bursts. No sooner does he reseal the windows, than the heat breaks down and the cold of the winter creeps into the place, freezing the pipes, and forcing him to walk around the house in scarves and mittens. The budget his employer provides him is inadequate to meet all these needs and so he finds himself spending his evenings writing lengthy letters begging, cajoling, and explaining why he needs an emergency transfer of more funds. His employer sends the money grudgingly. There are veiled threats that, if he can't decrease the cost of the work, another caretaker will be found. But now the urinals in the large basement bathroom are clogged, the electricity has burned out in the kitchen, causing a small fire that destroyed the industrial-sized stove situated there, and the boiler, a truly ancient machine, requires constant attention. He spends a considerable number of his hours trying to keep it running or observing it to make sure that it is running as it should. Yet, no matter how hard he works, and he works at an increasingly frantic pace, sleeping less and less every night, the decay continues to accelerate. He begins to wonder if he is Sisyphus, trapped in a hell of eternally recurring labor devoid of any reward.

And then strange things start happening. Perhaps it is due to his lack of sleep, but he begins to find windows open that he knew were closed,

The Third Part: Fatherland

doors closed that he knew were open, and taps, taps like those in the row of three child-sized bathtubs on the second floor, left open with the water running. He begins to hear footsteps in hallways where no people are present, unsettling noises coming from the basement, and he swears the swing in the orchard is moving on a windless day. This is only the beginning as his periods of sleeplessness and frantic work, paired with equally frantic letter writing, continue to accumulate. He begins to see children in the buildings and on the grounds—here is one disappearing into the doorway of a room, here is another in the loft of the barn, here is a third under his bed. They are all poorly clothed; many not wearing much more than underwear. But, every time he goes looking for them, or checks a second time, they are gone. Still, the presence of the children gradually increases and he begins to believe they are gathering in the orchard at night, climbing down the sheer brick walls of the house, passing by his window. Strange murmurings reach his ears.

"Satonhkária'ks kénh?"
"Hén, katonhkári'ks."
"Wahiákon ki sewahió:wane."

The buildings continue to decay. The boiler continues to attract his attention.

And then the children begin to change. Health young bodies now appear twisted, broken, limping. On the porch, he encounters a girl with blood coming out of her ears. In the orchard, there is a boy whose back is covered with lacerations. And on the floor in an old playroom, he finds a girl with a battered face, covered in welts, having a seizure. He runs to fetch water and when he returns to her, she is gone. One day, while fixing the chicken wire that was pulled up in the night, he hears the sounds of a belt slapping against flesh, followed each time by a small boy's cries, coming from within the chicken coop. The tone of the children also changes. Now, instead of laughing and fleeing from him they begin to scream and yell. They become more corporeal and they become more hostile. Instead of gathering in the orchard at night, he believes they are now gathering in the hallway outside his door whispering and clustering, like spiders, on the wall outside his window.

"Boozhoo."
"Aaniin."
"Aanii piish enjebayin?"

A Magnificent Work

"Aamjiwnaang ndojeba."
"Aaniin endaso-biboonagiziyan?"
"Zhaangaswi. Aaniin endaso-diba' iganed?"
"Ashi niizho-diba' iganed."
"Ogichidaakweg?"
"Eya' Ogichidaakweg."

He notices that many of them now have blood staining their underwear and dripping down their thighs. He discovers they will not enter the boiler room and so he begins sleeping there. It becomes increasingly difficult to maintain the buildings and grounds. He writes again to his employer for help, but no help is forthcoming. Instead, he is told that he will receive no further warnings and, if he cannot do his job adequately with the "more than ample resources provided," he will be replaced. Truly, he concludes, I am in hell.

So, he decides to take matters into his own hands. Encountering a cluster of children on a landing, he charges them and discovers that they are now fully real and that he can hit them and that he, as a man, a very tall man, is much larger and stronger than them. He beats them and they run screaming up the stairs. Soon, he is hunting them. He nearly drowns a girl in a bucket of water he was using to clean windows. He discovers that this delights him. He hangs a boy from one of the pipes in the basement and beats him. He laughs afterwards and reenacts the scene in the boiler room that night before going to sleep. He begins to neglect his work and parts of the house and the other buildings begin to collapse as the rot never ceases to progress. The barn caves in. Wallpaper begins to peel. The entire south stairwell becomes unusable. The lawn is overgrown. He writes fabricated reports to his employer, "I believe that I finally have a handle on everything and, having completed all the major repairs, I am now comfortably maintaining the grounds at the standard of cleanliness and dignity that they deserve." He plots his next hunt. Instead of simply fighting the children, he makes a trap to capture one. His plan is successful and he takes the child captive in the boiler room with him. He captures many of them. They all go into the boiler room with him, but none of them come out. He grows taller and taller. The children seem smaller and smaller, younger and younger. His employer is content. This is not hell, he realizes. For me, this is heaven. It is the children, laughs the Wendigo, who are in hell.

And so I awoke.

12

CHILDREN AT THE MOHAWK Institute were not permitted to speak their own languages.[1] If they did so, they were beaten or punished in some other equally abusive fashion (the only real limits to the brutality of the staff members were the limits of their imagination—for example, at another Indian Residential school in Ontario, St. Anne's, staff members made an electric chair that they used to torture children, sometimes to the amusement of the local townspeople who would come and watch what it was capable of doing to a child, some of whom were as young as 6 when it was used on them).[2] Depriving a people of its language, it one of the surest ways of exterminating it. When a language dies, so does a culture, a way of being in the world, and a lens through which things are appreciated and understood. Words create worlds, and destroying a people's words does not only destroy that people's world, it also destroys them as *that* people. It makes them something else. And this is how "Indians," how "pagans, heathens, and savages" were to be transformed into "Canadians" and "Christians."

Every morning, the children were required to say the Lord's Prayer.[3] I imagine many of them learned it phonetically first. The very limited education the children received, little more than an hour or two a day, also took place in English (one teacher delighted in holding children's heads

---

1. See Graham, *The Mush Hole*, 22, 380, 410.

2. For one survivor account of the horrors that occurred at St. Anne's, see Metatawabin with Shimo, *Up Ghost River*. In terms of the genocidal brutality of the Indian Residential schools as a system, see Starblanket, *Suffer the Little Children*.

3. On the history of religious indoctrination developed as a substitute for education at the Mohawk Institute see Library and Archives of Canada. School File Series—1879–1953 (RG 10-B-3-d), C-7933-00672; C-7933-00689; C-7933-00704; C-7933-00721; C-7933-00763; C-7933-00801; C-7933-00819; C-7933-00845; C-7933-00904; C-7933-00960; C-7933-00967; C-7933-00994; C-7933-01032; C-7933-010136; C-7933-01073; C-7933-01223; C-7933-01252.

underwater in a bucket that she kept by her desk, and which she used if the children misspoke; on one occasion, she very nearly drowned a girl). The education was not aligned with provincial standards for curriculum. Instead, it was increasingly devoted to Christian indoctrination and, once again, the Lord's Prayer was prominent. Many students who spent years at the Institute—say from the age of 6 to 18—came away from the school with little more than a third-grade level of literacy and numeracy.

Instead, manual labor dominated the days.[4] The girls were required to engage in domestic duties like cooking, cleaning, and sewing, in order to prepare themselves to be dutiful wives (they were only permitted out of the building for one hour a day and, even then, had to stay within a fenced-in enclosure). The boys were required to engage in all manners of farm labor. This was often demanding and led one doctor to comment on the very unusual and extremely high number of hernias he was diagnosing in the children. Another result of this was that the staff members were constantly eating fresh farm produce—fruits, vegetables, butter, eggs—while the children were eating mush.[5] Although milk was abundant, due to the presence of a large number of dairy cows, the children were only given improperly stored and unpasteurized skim milk. This was an ongoing cause of concern and frustration for medical examiners who, with the backing of Superintendents from Indian Affairs, continually order the Principals to provide the children with fresh, healthy, pasteurized milk. These orders are ignored and continue to be ignored even after the Principals are warned that their intransigence is not only unethical but also illegal.[6] It was well known that unpasteurized and improperly stored milk can contain bacteria like E. Coli, Salmonella, Listeria, Brucella, Campylobacter, and Cryptosporidium, any of which could produce a potentially fatal health crisis in a malnourished, improperly dressed, and traumatized child.

Still, every day, the children recited:

---

4. As one survivor notes, "I was just a slave . . . It was like a concentration camp" (as quoted in Graham, *The Mush Hole*, 399). The manual labour involved was also emphasised in the conversation I had with Jessica Powless in December 2016, and with Virve Wiland and Amos Key Jr., in January and February, 2017.

5. See Graham, *The Mush Hole*, 388.

6. This issue appears repeatedly in the records. See, for example, Library and Archives of Canada. School File Series—1879–1953 (RG 10-B-3-d), C-7933-01309; C-7933-01875; C-7933-02155; C-7935-00055.

The Third Part: Fatherland

> Our Father, who art in heaven
> hallowed by thy name;
> thy kingdom come;
> thy will be done;
> On earth as it is in heaven.
> Give us this day our daily bread.
> And forgive us our trespasses,
> as we forgive those who trespass against us.
> And lead us not into temptation;
> but deliver us from evil.
> For thine is the kingdom,
> the power and the glory,
> for ever and ever.
> Amen.

When Europeans settlers first began to colonize Turtle Island, they often remarked on two things: how local parents did not use corporal punishment as a tool for teaching or disciplining their children, and how the people, in general, lacked any concept of "hell" or "the fear of god." One missionary with the New England Company recounts a story about how, after telling some Inuit people about the fires of hell, he discovers, much to his dismay, that they want directions so that they can go and warm themselves there.[7] Survivors of the Mohawk Institute recall the Sunday sermons in Her Majesty's Chapel of the Mohawks as being "all fire and brimstone."[8] To help illustrate this point, one Sunday morning, a boy who had run away and been found hiding in the City dump was brought into the chapel and made to sit at the front where all the other children could observe him.[9] He was covered with impetigo, and his tongue was purple and swollen out of his mouth because, it was reported, it had been bitten by a rat. The children, after receiving this warning, were made to sing *Onward Christian Soldiers*. Still, the fear of god did not come easily. Corporal punishment, torture, abduction, rape, the mass deaths of one's siblings, friends, and peers, and going away to an Institute where the odds of you coming back alive were 50/50, accomplished what theological lessons had not. Ritualized abuse was the true liturgy of the Mohawk Institute. It was designed to produce young bodies that were marked and habituated by the belief that they were

---

7. Hitchin and the Governor and Court of the New England Company, *'Come Over and Help Us,'* 9.

8. As related to me in conversation with a personal friend in 2017.

9. For the story that follows, see Graham, *The Mush Hole*, 381.

A Magnificent Work

morally and ontologically inferior heathens and savages, dirty and impure, in need of salvation and transformation into a superior way of being: that of Christian Canadians. And so, just as acts of violence accumulate and culminate in the tenure of a Principal who received the honorary name "Skin," the number of hours dedicated to religious instruction in the Institute also steadily increases over its history. Thus, from the 1930s onwards, the following schedule is observed: morning prayers, three hours of class room teaching, now solely dedicated to religious instruction, evening chapel six days a week, and two chapel services on Sunday. Yet still Skin laments, "Since coming to the Institute one of the great disappointments has been the lack of time which I have been able to give to religious education."[10] But the lessons provided by teachers, by the Principals and Reverends and Chaplains and Townspeople, by the RCMP and the Government of Canada, by all these men and women of god, were not lost on the children. They learned the fear of god, their Father in heaven.

In an unexpected moment of candor, prompted by yet another medical report about unpasteurized milk, Superintendent Randle, observes the following:

> No-one knowing well the conditions of the Mohawk Institute can by happy or satisfied, or feel it is a credit to Indian Administration, or a place you could at any time show people over. Personally, it is my opinion—as is it is now almost purely a Departmental responsibility and the only Residential School serving a large number of populus [sic] Reserves, and must be maintained, the sooner we recognize this, the better. It should be a model of what a Residential School can be—a pleasure to see and go into, a place which turns out happy healthy Indian children ready to face the world, instead of a crowd who by the very environment in which they have lived and grown up in, have an inferiority complex often never overcome.[11]

---

10. Library and Archives of Canada. School File Series—1879–1953 (RG 10-B-3-d), C-7933-00908.

11. Library and Archives of Canada. School File Series—1879–1953 (RG 10-B-3-d), C-7933-01880-82

13

MY FATHERLAND, IN HIS own defense, has often said that although he may not have been a good father, at least now he is sorry and would like to pursue reconciliation. At least he broke that cycle. But my fatherland, my fatherland has always been a liar. And one thing I know about lying is this: there is nothing people lie about more than the things that they are incapable of admitting to themselves about themselves.

Or maybe he is playing games with truth. Maybe he really does feel sorry. Maybe He does want forgiveness or, at the very least, want everyone—even those he is killing—to like him. Maybe, in this way, he speaks the truth while lying.

("I killed her because I love her—is it too much to ask her, with her dying breath, to say 'I love you, too?'")

Regardless, a lie told often enough soon becomes a truth. To the teller first of all (because it is the teller who is most desperately in need of believing it) and so, perhaps, after all these years, my fatherland believes himself. I know that we believed him for a very long time.

I don't believe him anymore.

14

As told to Elizabeth Graham:

Once around Christmas, the Kiwanis club or one of them, gave a Christmas party and we were elected to go, and we were given toys. When we come back they stood up there, took the toys away from us and gave us socks—thin socks not work socks. Zimmerman and his wife and Miss Chisholm—she was the nurse—they would line up there and take them all away from us and give us socks. Dress socks—they were not good for work. They were useless, literally useless to us. They said the toys were no good to us, but they were—they were given to us . . . When the Queen became Queen, the Government gave us medals—they took 'em away from us. They were sent from the Government for us and they took 'em. I don't know what they did with them, but by rights they still belong to us. What Skin and his wife or those people did with them, whether they give them away or sold them; his children played with them—they might still have them. I don't know if they were gold plated or what but they were pretty anyway. Today the Church is not owning up to the problems—an apology. Rather than an apology they could give me back my toy. I wouldn't be happier than if they'd give me my toy back and my medal. An apology is like a voice on a windy day.[1]

---

1. Graham, *The Mush Hole*, 401.

Third Intermission

ON BATTLING GIANTS: A POEM FOR MY YOUNGEST BROTHER ON THE OCCASION OF HIS BIRTHDAY

WE RIDE BICYCLES UNTIL the trails end and follow creeks to culverts, under roads, far away, vast domains. At night, you are a king in a castle and I am a knight in a tower. We battle giants and talk with dragons. In the winter, we go to school along a road with no sidewalks. The slush and ice from the plows are often as deep as our knees. I walk on the side closest to the cars because you are my little brother and it is part of me to try and keep you safe.

And I try but you have always been courageous. Hitting ramps on rollerblades, crashing and scraping and bleeding and going back again, over and over again, until you had learned how to fly and how to land. Standing up to the bully who was mocking the knock-kneed kid in class who never bothered anyone. Doing the flips I was always too scared to try on a trampoline. And now, trying to wring some good out of massive institutions, convinced that you can be a part of making the world a better place, convinced that things don't have to be this way, convinced that they can be changed, convinced that you are changing them—you are still battling giants and you are doing so optimistically.

But still, in my heart, I want to keep you safe.

At the start of high school, it was you who first introduced me to the people who would become my friends. In our room, after our parents had kicked me out, you put up pictures and items on my now empty bed, as an act of grieving, love, remembrance, and rebellion. In all my years of talking to people about the ways in which lives are devastated by homelessness, you were one of the few who listened and took it all very seriously. And when I forgot my keys and came home late from work and was terrified to ring the bell or knock because I didn't want to wake my father and face his wrath,

A Magnificent Work

you were the one who opened the door after I threw gravel at our bedroom window. You weren't too happy about it, but you did it.

In your heart, you want to keep us all safe.

I know this, although your heart has often been a mystery to me. A mystery and a wonder. This man who speaks with quiet confidence was a king inside a castle, this professor being quoted by scholars and journalists was a boy using tap water to part his hair in the middle, this advocate calling for love and attention to the most vulnerable members of our community was sleeping beside me at our grandparents, making blanket forts, barricades of pillows, mountains and river valleys in the bed sheets. We created lives, we created worlds, we created safe spaces and love—we created them out of nothing.

And you haven't stopped. Only now the blanket forts you build are other people who care, and programs, policies and community development projects for people experiencing poverty, people experiencing homelessness, and people experiencing domestic violence. I'm proud of you, Giantslayer. I love you. You've got this.

(But if you ever get tired, if you ever feel doubt, if you ever feel you don't, I'll happily take the side of the road closest to the cars for a little while more.)

The Fourth Part

Land

"While writing about landscape often begins in the aesthetic, it must always tend to the ethical. [Barry] Lopez's attentiveness [in his book, *Arctic Dreams*] was, I came to later realize, a form of moral gaze, born of his belief that if we attend more closely to something then we are less likely to act selfishly towards it. To exercise a care of attention toward a place—as towards a person—is to achieve a sympathetic intimacy with it."[1]

---

1. MacFarlane, *Landmarks*, 211.

1

I.

Fossil stromatolites are a kind of sedimentary rock formed by the growth of layer upon layer of cyanobacteria.[1] Cyanobacteria are prokaryotes—single-celled organisms that lack things like a nucleus or mitochondria. Fossil evidence of their existence goes back about 3.7 billion years to the Archean Eon. That is to say, cyanobacteria existed before eukaryotes appeared (before the existence of single-celled organisms possessing a nucleus and other things like mitochondria—and mitochondria, too, once existed independently but made exponentially more complex and diverse forms of life possible once they became incorporated into cells). Cyanobacterium is the oldest known form of life we are aware of on earth.

By way of comparison, the oldest known rock on earth, a faux-amphibolite from the Nuvvuagittuq greenstone belt is about 4.28 billion years old, dating to the Hadean Eon. It formed at a time when the crust of the earth was very thin and prone to being destroyed by shifting plates, endless waves of asteroids, and constant volcanic eruptions (the earth itself is about 4.6 billion years old and a collision with a Mars-sized planetoid broke what became the moon off of the earth approximately 4.5 billion years ago).

The evidence we have from cyanobacteria suggests that life was already widespread and diverse 3.7 billion years ago, leading scientists to postulate that life itself was present here well before that time. However, cyanobacteria have contributed to the development of life on earth in several ways, including two that are very significant. First, the primordial oceans of the earth, produced by rainstorms that sometimes lasted for millennia,

---

1. See Hickman, "How have bacteria contributed to the evolution of multicellular animals?," 3–33; also Golubic, "Microbial Mats of Abu Dhabi," 103–30; and Golubic, "Stromatolites of Shark Bay," 131–47.

were, at that time, largely anoxic, as was the atmosphere. But cyanobacteria produced oxygen (it is the only known photosynthetic prokaryote capable of doing this) that went into the air and water and started the process of producing an oxygen rich environment. Secondly, cyanobacteria became essential to the evolution of plant life as the chloroplasts by which plants make food for themselves are actually cyanobacteria that began living within plant cells through a process of endosymbiosis during the Proterozoic Eon (which began 3.5 billion years ago).[2] The emerald green sea slug, Elysia Chlorotica, continues this process of endosymbiosis in salt marshes and shallow pools along the eastern coast of Turtle Island today, when, after feeding on Vaucheria litorea algae, it incorporates chloroplasts from that algae into its own genetic code.[3] This enables it to photosynthesize and feed on light. Over time, living things don't simply evolve, they also move in and out of each other and it is hard, increasingly hard depending on how far or close you are, to determine where one kind of life stops and another kind of life begins.

And yet, through all of this, the cyanobacteria persist. The oldest known fossil, a species that is 3.46 billion years older than the first dinosaurs, a species older than all multicellular organisms, continues to flourish today in a world unrecognizably and unimaginably different than that of the Archaean Eon. Commonly referred to as blue-green algae and present everywhere from geysers in Yellowstone, to ocean waters, to Icelandic hot springs, studies are now suggesting that consuming (incorporating into ourselves?) certain species of cyanobacteria help humans manage cholesterol, inflammation, heart disease and nonalcoholic fatty liver disease. Because we, too, are products of endosymbiosis. We, too, are endosymbionts and ecosystems. This is true even at the level of our DNA. More than one third of human genes have their origins in bacteria and at least eight percent of our DNA, that stuff we tell ourselves is the core of who we uniquely are as homo sapiens, is composed of non-human viral fragments.[4]

II.

After I cross the Deshkan Ziibiing, I cut left and wrap back around to the riverbank and go under the bridge. The paved walkway curls around to the

2. See Archibald, *One Plus One Equals One*.
3. See Sultan, *Organism and Environment*, 32–33.
4. See Cordingley, *Viruses*, 275–98.

sidewalk on the other side of the street but, if you veer off to the right, as I do, there is the tiniest patch of undeveloped, uncultivated land. There used to be houses and a parking lot here but they were torn down and torn up and the land was left alone. The trees line the river, only about half a dozen deep, but if you follow the path, you can find just enough space to imagine that you are not in a city. The path is at the foot of a small but steep hill, which is likely no more than nine feet at its highest point. Another path cuts diagonally across the abandoned patch of land and, in the growing seasons, tall grasses, wildflowers, and other plants sprout and grow as tall as me. In the spring, I brush them with my fingertips. The dew soaks into my pants. Other creatures return to inhabit the space year after year. Sparrows and mallards. Once, a heron in the shallows, standing like a statue of a prehistoric creature. Another time, two deer moving silently through the underbrush. Once, even a beaver spent a few days on this section of river seeming, to me, to be a bit lost and confused. Rarely, fish jumping in a river that feels as devastated and as peaceful as a clear-cut. I learn to listen to the soundscape of the birds and insects, things that we have forgotten how to hear because we have trained ourselves to ignore the constant noise pollution of city life.

(When the machines and spinners and presses and fires of the first factories in England came to life, villagers and others living in the countryside, even those miles away, would complain that the noise the inventions generated fractured and shattered their manner of living. Now we take it all this noise so much for granted that we don't hear it. Noise pollution, light pollution, chemical pollution, we forget them all, just like we forget that only a few years ago, no more than the blink of an eye really, people used to come and drink from this river that now smells of pesticides and sewage.)

Walking the same path, year after year as I have done for six years now, one begins to get a sense for the rhythms of place. The rise of the river in the Autumn, its freezing in the winter, coming to life in the Spring, and idling in the summer; which way the wind blows in the morning and the afternoon in springtime, and which way the wind blows in the morning and the afternoon in the Autumn. One begins to develop a sense of connectedness. A sense of belonging. A sense of attachment to and communion with other forms of life—the sun that rises over the river, the river itself, the trees that stand like guardians at the entrance of the path, the snake who left her skin in the stones by the sidewalk, the birds and flowers and creeping things. If one were to do this for generations, for hundreds or thousands of years as the Indigenous peoples of this land have done, I wouldn't be surprised if this attachment was, somehow, coded into one's DNA. We're only just beginning to learn about epigenetics, DNA methylation, and the porousness of organisms and environments.[5]

Once a year, on this small plot of land, there is a great birth and migration of snails (gastropods from the mollusk phylum, kin of emerald green sea slug). They travel south to north across the path and climb high up onto the grasses. I don't know why they do this. I wonder if sitting atop the grass makes them easier targets for birds but I also wonder what awaits them on the ground below, and I wonder how they feel about the shade or the sun on their shells. The babies would easily fit onto the nail of my pinky finger. There are far too many of them to be numbered. I step carefully so as not to crush them. I don't know where they come from or where they are going but, every year, they are there and I say thank you to them and I marvel at their beauty and I try to imagine how a snail prays and what kinds of songs they sing, and how distant and small the earth below must look from atop a blade of grass.

But now signs have gone up that the land has been rezoned (you can call City Hall at the number provided if you have any questions), one of the trees I love and loved has been cut down, and the patch of land is driven over by machines, riding mowers, once or twice in the Spring and Summer. The men on the machines wear industrial ear protection because of the amount of noise they generate. And there are no longer any snails. They have vanished, although I still find old shells in the mud down by the water's edge. I wonder where they have gone. There used to be so many of them. I wonder if anyone else has noticed or mourned their absence. Because I have and I do.

III.

We have killed, or are in the midst of killing, everything that filled me with wonder when I was a child. The Western Black Rhinoceros is extinct. The effective population of Amur Tigers in the wild is now somewhere between 27 and 35 and there haven't been any Java Tigers, none at all, since I was 14. Lonesome George, the last Pinta Island Tortoise, died on June 14, 2012,

---

5. Regarding epigenetics and DNA methylation refer to Jablonka and Lamb, *Evolution in Four Dimensions*, 111–52; Zimmer, *She Has Her Mother's Laugh*, 422–44; and throughout.

The Fourth Part: Land

after one hundred years of solitude. The Yangtze River Dolphin was finally completely exterminated in 2006 and a singularly beautiful species of snail in Malaysia stopped existing in 2014 when a transnational concrete company blew up the only limestone hill in the world where the snails lived. Due to coastal logging, which has now cut deep enough to prevent the inland transfer of water accomplished by the respiration of trees, the death of the entire Amazon rainforest is now assured. That forest was once called "the lungs of the planet" because it produced more than 20% of the world's oxygen. Of the approximately 10 million species of plants, animals, and insects, we have collected and catalogued (in museums, in pictures, in mortuaries), more than half call that forest home. It used to cover 7% of the earth's dry land (2% of the earth's surface). It's hard to miss, even from space, but I miss it already. I also miss another massive life form that is visible from space, because obituaries have now been published for the Great Barrier Reef, that once living thing, that once living multitude of things, now bleached and bleaching like bones in the sun.

We can use all kinds of language for this—extinct, vanished, dead, gone, exterminated, stopped existing—but the truth is that all these lives and forms of life were murdered. They were murdered. They were murdered by the small number of people who had the ability to kill them and who found it profitable to do so. Many people were involved in this and benefited from it, but a more precise reckoning would place most of the blame on the shoulders of a few. Less than one percent of the approximately 7.6 billion people who are alive today.

Our population has been exploding but, as of 2011, it was estimated that the total number of homo sapiens who have ever lived on earth up until that point, was 108 billion. In comparison to this, scientists have estimated that the number of bacterial cells living in a single human body fluctuate between 30 and 50 trillion (working off of averages based on my body weight, I expel approximately 400 times more bacteria from my body in bowel movements over a twenty-four hour period than the number of humans who have ever lived).[6]

And so I have fled to the very small (and the very large) because I need wonder to live. And I need to know that we or they (the less than 1%) can't kill the sum total of we, the living. And we or they can't. There are just as many species of bacteria on earth as all the known species of plants,

---

6. For popular studies of the human microbiome see DeSalle and Perkins, *Welcome to the Microbiome*; and Yong, *I Contain Multitudes*.

animals, and insects (not to mention the 209 known species of Archaeans) and, if we count viruses as a form of life (and I do), well, there are possibly 100 million different kinds of viruses, and that estimate doesn't count the viruses that operate solely in the domain of prokaryotes (to say nothing of weird life and the possibility of a shadow biome).[7] The cyanobacteria have been here since the dawn of life as we, in our very limited way, recognize it here on this living thing, this multitude of living things, we call earth. And the cyanobacteria will still be here long after us. And in five billion years, when the hydrogen in the sun is depleted and its helium begins to fuse with carbon causing the sun to rapidly expand, even though it is collapsing in on itself because the force of gravity is no longer balanced by the force of fusion, it will be the cyanobacteria who are eventually and utterly changed into fire and light. Homo sapiens, like the Western Black Rhinoceros and Lonesome George, will be long gone.

---

7. See Davies, *The Eerie Silence*, 42–65.

2

In June of 2015, I went to Iceland. On the first day, I stood looking over mountains covered in fog (clouds blown in from the North Atlantic) and volcanic fields covered in moss (moss as thick as pillows) and a blue-green lake that had formed in a crater caused by a geothermal explosion (Graenvatn, just south of Krýsuvík within the Reykjanesfólkvangur) and I raised my hands and stretched them out as far as I could reach and I spoke without knowing what I was going to speak and I said, "I belong in the earth." And I was surprised by what I spoke, but even in the midst of my surprise, I knew that those words, in all their newness to me, were exactly what I wanted and what I wanted to say.

    I belong in the earth.

3

I.

In September, 2013, I attended a funeral for a young man I knew from my work. He died in a bed in a homeless shelter. He was barely over thirty but, in many ways, he was still a child. His brain didn't work the same as most other people's brains work. Some of his family members showed up for the funeral—it was my first time seeing any of them in the two years that I knew this fellow—and they put together a montage of pictures from his childhood. He looks sweet and happy and maybe a little bit awkward. He, too, got his heart broken along with his mind . . . although I'm never sure if minds that we consider broken actually are, or if we are the ones with broken minds, or if all of us have broken minds, in which case, I'm not sure why it matters to emphasize the brokenness of some minds over others. Regardless, his body broke as well and then he never got up again. He went from laying in his bed to laying in a stretcher to laying on a slab to laying in a coffin. I felt like I was attending the funeral of a child and it made me weep. He often made me laugh, with the accents he would assume when he spoke, with the way he pretended to shoot us with his fingers, "Bang! Bang!" and with the ways he was constantly sneaking in and out of places he was told not to go. This, too, is a child like my son, I kept thinking, this, too, is a child like my daughter. And he is dead, he is dead, he has been carried away, and we will never see him again.

(Nietzsche said that God is dead and we have killed him, but he neglected to mention that all of us on the way to becoming superheroes are killing children, too.)

At the funeral, the priest—the family asked for a Catholic service of sorts—talked about God's love and how this young man was welcomed home to heaven where he was being embraced by the love of God . . . and

The Fourth Part: Land

I wept because of this, too. It's such a beautiful story and I remember how beautiful the world was when I believed that story, but now I don't know what to believe.

I do know this—this young man was the fourth "street person" that I knew who died in a five-week period. People are dying faster here than I remember them dying elsewhere. All this, despite the City Managers and public advocates and professional service providers, who talk about how they are "curing" homelessness in this town. I've noticed that these people like to talk about poverty and health and the public good, but none of them seem to talk about oppression. Until they do, people will continue to die here.

III.

As all these people were dying, I got word from a dear friend out West that the eight-year-old son of one of her dear friends had been diagnosed with inoperable brain cancer. They cut the kid's head open once to try and remove the cancer, but they weren't able to get all of it. He's in a hospital room confused and frightened and in a lot of pain when his meds start wearing off. His mom is barely holding on with the help of booze and pills and a loving husband and a loving friend.

This child is eight years old. Can we understand this? The world is full of parents grieving the loss of the children and children grieving the loss of their parents and lovers grieving the loss of their friends and all of us grieving, deep in our bones, everything that has been taken away before its time. If we start from this recognition—form acknowledging this grief in all of us—where do we end up?

(At the time of the funeral, I was rereading *The Brothers Karamazov* and I was struck by the words of Father Zossima when he tells Alyosha to hold himself responsible for all the sin in the world and hold himself accountable to all the pain in the world—to take it into himself and carry it as his own. My God, I thought, I made the mistake of taking that advice seriously. It's terrible advice. Don't do it. It's unbearable.)

IV.

At the same time, another dear friend of mine told me his marriage had fallen apart. He has been very involved, from the very beginning, with a lot of the Truth and Reconciliation work taking place in Vancouver. When I was at my lowest point there, I was a poor friend to him but he was a good friend to me, and he took me in for a time and gave me a home and was kind and gentle and considerate with and to me. I remember sitting in his kitchen and watching him make peanut butter and jam sandwiches for his kids. He was a fantastic sandwich maker. He did everything just the way the kids wanted it done and he did it like it was nothing at all, chatting happily with me all the while. I remember thinking, "I hope, one day, to be the kind of father you are."

But now he, too, has been abandoned. Now he, too, will only see his kids part-time. This, too, seems like an unbearable thought.

V.

In the summer of 2013, I started talking to the flowers and the trees when I walked to work in the morning. I thanked them for being beautiful, I thanked them for giving us clean air to breathe and for replenishing the soil and for caring for the bees and ants and creeping things. I apologized to them for the ways we are poisoning them. I apologized to them for cutting down their brothers and sisters (the City recently felled a number of old trees that I used to pass on my morning route). I told them that I didn't know what to do to make things better. I touched their skins—their bark and leaves—I felt the dew and rain that collected on them and rubbed the water into my palms. I smelled the evergreens. I asked them to come and visit me in my dreams, where we can share a common tongue and speak with one another and be understood.

What do you see when you look upon the world into which you have been thrown? What are you looking for? What do you find there?

For a long time, I went looking for Death. Not because I was attracted to Death but because I thought that love could conquer Death and I thought that I could be an agent of love and Life in places abandoned and scarred and living the valley of the shadow of Death.

And I found Death. The more I looked, the more I found Death everywhere. I found him lurking under jungle gyms in suburban parks. I saw him pissing behind a tree on the trails by UBC. Once, I passed him while he was smoking a cigarette at the base of the war memorial in Victory Square. I grew up with him, as did many others. The kids and adults and men and women I have worked with over the years were intimately acquainted with him. I hung out in dive bars he frequented—bars that put up signs saying, "watch your drinks, date rapes happen here." I hung out in high-end bars where he came just as frequently but nobody put up any signs.

Death does not discriminate. I found him in the company of the rich and I found him in the company of the poor. He was in dining rooms and conference centers and churches and alleys and condos and greasy spoon breakfast joints and everywhere, if you know where to look. He asked thoughtful questions, he listened to lonely people talk, he often sat in silence watching us, he was generous with his embrace. He was nothing but generous.

So, I looked for Death and I found him and I thought that love would conquer him . . . but slowly and inexorably, Death conquered me. I grew tired. I stopped loving well. And then I forgot what it is to love. Love became a stranger to me . . . and I became more and more attracted to Death.

Memento mori, memento mori, memento mori—how could I forget?

VI.

That summer, I would sit on my couch and look out the window of my apartment. All I could see were the trees and the sky. It was that summer when I realized that trees are alive—they are a form of life, silently growing and breathing and eating and drinking, just outside my window. I began to count how many I could see and I lost track somewhere around fifty. My god, I realized, I am surrounded by Life. I looked at the flowers. I looked at all the tiny blades of grass growing from the lawn below me. My god, my god, Life is so abundant. It's everywhere. Silently there. Silently alive.

The world is full of Life.

My daughter already understood this. When I held her up to the window, she would laugh and smile and point and do an excited wriggle in my arms every time we spotted something. That summer, we saw squirrels and skunks and raccoons and rabbits and dogs and cats and geese and mallards and hawks and sparrows and starlings and cardinals and red-winged blackbirds and chickadees and butterflies and spiders and beetles and ants and one groundhog.

And that was the summer when I was finally able to cry again, for the first time in four years, for the first time since I cried outside of the security clearance at Vancouver's airport saying goodbye, I started crying again counting trees or looking for birds with my daughter, because life had begun to feel like a gift again.

VII.

The months passed and I continued to talk with the birds and the trees and the river and the grass and the bugs and the bushes and the flowers when I walked to work in the morning. I continued to invite them to meet me in my dreams, although they never did but then, one day, something happened. They spoke back.

I had just finished speaking my invitation to my dreams when I realized that I didn't need to wait for my dreams to hear what they were saying to me. And then two words appeared in my mind like a thought that was not a thought, at least not my thought, or an idea that was not an idea, at least not my idea, it was more like a two-word sensation. And these were those words:

"Be grateful."

That was all. Be grateful. And at first, I was confused because, in many ways, since that summer, I had been feeling far more grateful than I had felt in years. But, as I thought about it more, I thought perhaps they were recommending that I be grateful even for the things for which I am not usually grateful. And then I thought about how I also apologize to the plants and the animals and the river and the soil every day because I am counted among those who are poisoning and killing them all. And this is what I thought they were saying:

> We know that we are sick. But every day we continue to sing, we continue to flow, we continue to bloom. We know that we are dying and that you have poisoned us. But every day we choose to offer ourselves as something beautiful and good to the world. We don't want your apologies. We know you're sorry and we know you can't make it better. Stop saying sorry and start saying thank you.

And then I thought about the kid with brain cancer and I thought about other kids who are dying and I thought about how they still draw pictures and they still sing songs and they still dance and they still tell stories, while they still can, and they don't want us to spend all our time crying over them and saying, "I'm sorry, I'm sorry, I'm sorry." Instead, they want us to say, "My god, what a beautiful picture. Thank you! It's perfect, I love it—can I have another?"

And so I have started to say that.

4

AT SKÓGAFOSS I LEFT behind the tourists with their cameras, cell phones, tablets, and other personal electronic devices, and followed the gravel bed beside the Skógar up to the little pool at the base of the falls. Five meters in front of the last pair of tourists, the spray had already soaked me through my jacket. Ten meters beyond that, the spray was so intense that it felt as though I was walking through a cloudburst and I had to squint my eyes in order to be able to see anything at all. But this is what I saw: a rainbow that formed in a circle around me and that grew ever brighter the deeper into the spray I went. I gasped and laughed and wondered what else we might see if we spent more time going where we can't take pictures. I continued moving forward. As I approached the limits of the land and of the visible, where air and water and space and motion all swirled increasingly closer together, and my laughter was inaudible, even to me, because of the roar of the falls, and the rainbow shone brighter than any HDTV, a second rainbow formed around the first one.

And when my marriage was dying and I was soothing my sorrows with alcohol, I spent many nights in dive bars and I learned to appreciate the Stones. But, despite what Mick proclaims in the song, "Blinded by Rainbows," it was only after I journeyed passed the screaming, through the pain, in a night that smelled of fear, that I was blinded by rainbows—baptized by rainbows, us children of light.

5

In my life and work, I have often remembered Victor Frankl's line, "What is to give light must endure burning."[1] It ties in well with others who have inspired me at different times—from Jesus's call to "take up your cross," to the Buddhist notion of the Bodhisattva, to Henri Nouwen's study of "the wounded healer."[2] But lately I have been thinking about fireflies which transform energy into light without producing heat. None of the energy is wasted; all that is produced is light.

Because, yes, there are any number of things worth dying for and any number of bodies or agencies or corporations willing to allow you to make that sacrifice or willing to take your life as they roll along and, yes, none of that invalidates the magnitude of the sacrifice involved and none of that is meant to suggest that all such struggles (or any such struggles) are hopeless and so, if you choose to die, there are many ways to die well. The via dolorosa is broad and many are those who walk it. Few deliberately and wholeheartedly choose it but, for those who do, their employers and elected officials and neighbors are happy to allow them to walk it until they can't anymore and someone else who is just as strong, just as noble, just as devoted, just as love-struck, takes their place.

As for me, I am tired of burning out and blowing up. I'm tired of dying. I'm tired of enduring burning. The fireflies suggest another way. They will never overpower the darkness but they can transform the night into something beautiful. And I would be content to
just
glow.

---

1. Frankl, *Man's Search for Meaning*, 69.
2. See Luke 9:23; Sangharakshita, *The Bodhisattva Ideal*; and Nouwen, *The Wounded Healer*.

6

The Waabshkaabkaag are a range of white orthoquartzite hills dating back about 2.5 billion years. What was once sand on the floor of a shallow sea was pressed into rock and thrust upwards 1.86 billion years ago. They formed mountains as tall as the Himalayas, before eons of erosion, including two million years of advancing and retreating ice ground them down to the hills they are today. We know them by the name they were given by European settlers because of the ways in which the Anishinaabe would strike boulders in the hills (one? several? it is hard to know) to make them ring alarm bells—it was always the sounds of warnings that greeted the coming of my people, and woe to those who had never needed to be warned before—but some say that the hills also rang for ceremony and to signal passing canoes. Northwest of here, by the Pukaskwa River, pits provide evidence that the Anishinaabe have been of this land for something in the range of 1,000 to 10,000 years. Evidence found to the southwest, near Sheguiandah on Manitoulin Island, suggest that 10,000 years may actually be a conservative estimate. Sites awaiting further exploration are also located close to what is now called George Lake in Killarney Provincial Park, including a white quartzite quarry that may date back 9,000 to 10,000 years. The people of this land are old. This land is old. Long before these hills were the La Cloche Mountains they have been, and continue to be, the Waabshkaabkaag. Long before that, no one knows what they were called. And long before that, they were before names. But perhaps, even then, the rocks sang.

Just to the south of the white quartzite hills, are ridges of pink granite and belts of red gneiss that formed during the Grenville Orogeny, some years after the Waabshkaabkaag rose from the primordial sea, and it was sitting in a thin layer of snow on Granite Ridge, looking to the north, across a valley of maple, birch, cedar and pine in the winter of 2017, that I realized that contentment is less in doing and more in being. The White Rocks

A Magnificent Work

simply are and, if you spend some time with them, you will realize that, because they are, they are content. And awakening to this is less like knowing and more like becoming—becoming Waabshkaabkaag, heat and pressure transforming broken pieces like grains of sand into rock into mountains, a spiritual orogeny, becoming content.

There are those who believe it is foolish to speak of hills being content, who think it unscientific to ascribe emotions to rocks, let alone a whole mountain range, and they may say this kind of anthropomorphism warps our ability to experience other things as they truly are and as truly other. But I think it is the epitome of our civilization's hubris to think that we, or a very small number of other things we have decided are like us (ravens, elephants, dogs), are the only things capable of feeling joy or sorrow, empathy or wonder.[1] Or love. I have felt the excitement of the Antlered River in the springtime when it was swollen in the first melt of the Spring and I, too, have been greeted by the river when I first called its name, "Deshkan Ziibiing! Deshkan Ziibiing! Deshkan Ziibiing!" and three large fish jumped out of the water, one after the other. When I was heartbroken it was the trees who taught me to be grateful and now, when I was mindbroken, it was the White Rocks who taught me contentment. Speaking in this way is not anthropocentric. It recognizes that, when it comes to feeling such things, we are omnimorphic. Our emotions do not set us apart from everything. They connect us with everything. We belong to the land and, like the land, we feel. If we forget that connection, if we lose that sense of belonging, we become sick. Our feelings become disarrayed and, like infants deprived of physical affection, we either die or develop in ways that make it difficult for us to connect meaningfully with others.

It is the same for all of life—hence the famous studies done of Rhesus monkeys deprived of maternal affection (we are always torturing animals only to discover that that they, like us, respond to torture in a tortured manner—infant Rhesus monkeys develop pathologies when deprived of affection, rats develop self-soothing patterns of obsessive substance use when separated from a meaningful connection to their peers or family members, and shrimp develop anxiety when submitted to a regimen of electric shocks and can have their anxiety treated with a common anti-anxiety medication), but we now know that trees also respond in a similar way. Trees that are transplanted as seedlings often struggle to have their roots network well with other roots in

---

1. For explorations of emotions felt by so-called "higher forms of life," see King, *How Animals Grieve*; and Safina, *Beyond Words*.

The Fourth Part: Land

the forest floor and, since trees often send food and messages to one another through their roots (with the assistance of the fungal networks that fill the soil—several miles of fungal filament can be contained within a single gram of soil), these transplanted trees remain socially isolated and become much more prone to illness and premature death.[2]

Connectedness and feelings, these are some of the basic building blocks of things that are. Because of our connectedness, we have made some lands sick and some lands discontent, but the Waabshkaabkaag are old and, although the sulphide ore smelters to the northeast acidified a number of the 600 or so lakes in Killarney in the mid to late twentieth century—lakes particularly vulnerable to this process because the orthoquartzite bedrock is so erosion resistant—annihilating, amongst other things, populations of fish, crustaceous zooplankton, amphibians, and mayflies, the White Rocks have about 2.5 billion years of perspective on these happenings. And, it seems, they remain content. Not disconnected. Not unfeeling. But content.

For many years, I focused on hurting with those who hurt, on mourning with those who mourn, on moving into the pain of others, the pain of the world. I felt responsible for it and accountable to it. I distrusted the apathy and actions of those who tried to avoid it or distance themselves from it. I felt as though I could not look away, there was blood on my hands (blood because I am male, blood because I am cishet, blood because I am middle-class, blood because I am white, blood because I am a settler, blood because I am Canadian), and so I owed it to the dead and murdered and taken and disappeared and tortured to look and see, to search out the videos and stories and histories, of all the violence that people like me have done in all the years that people like me have been. I thought this was a requirement of empathy, of love, of solidarity, of being-together-with others.

But you needn't research every little-known genocide—look, here are pictures and, look, here is a video—to learn what you need to learn about humans and genocide. You needn't watch every video of slaughtered elephants to learn about what humans do to other living things when money is involved. And you needn't read every account of rape, to learn about men and women or children and sex and power and violence and patriarchy. I think I've done my learning (although, as always, the proof of this will be the ways in which others experience me).

---

2. On this, and comments that follow about trees in subsequent chapters, see especially Wohlleben, *The Hidden Life of Trees*.

A Magnificent Work

When I went to the Waabshkaabkaag, I did not feel as if my sorrows, my worries, and my pain were ignored or invalidated. Instead, I felt as though I was in a place that felt like peace and that I, just as I was, was invited to partake in this peace. It felt very big and very old but it didn't feel invasive or overbearing. No more so than the sunrise feels invasive to those who have spent a night out sleeping in the cold. And, this, I realized is how I would like to be with others. I no longer want to be a repository of sorrows. I am not a coffin or a mass grave and I don't want to be surplus storage for the pain of the world. I'm far too small for that role anyway. Instead, like the White Rocks, the roots of ancient mountains, I want to be a vessel of peace. Bring your pain. We all are already, always carrying our pain with us, but, instead of me going away grieving, I want you to go away content.

7

I HADN'T REALIZED HOW much my senses had awakened in Iceland, where everything felt alive, the mountainsides covered with Lupins, the birds incessantly singing under the midnight sun, filling my water bottle from Gljúfrabúi or in Fjaðrárgljúfur or at the Fall of the Gods, until I returned home and discovered that my shower water smells of chlorine and the river that I love and call by name smells like shit and death and rotting things.

The same thing happened when I returned from the Waabshkaab-kaag, driving six hours down a highway, behind diesel trucks and pickups hauling quads back to the city (it was deer hunting season), breathing stale air pumped through vents, after spending three days and two nights in temperatures that rarely went above freezing and, on the first night, dropped down to negative twenty-four degrees Celsius. By the time I got off the highway, my sinuses were throbbing and I had a headache behind my eyes.

Living rocks, living water, living air, living fire, living wood, living forests, living mountains, living hills, there is so much life and, when we return to the living, we, too, come alive. But we can shut down just as quickly when we return to the world of our own making. I only smelled the chemicals in my shower water on the first day back. After that, the water just seemed to be water.

One hundred and fifty years ago, people drank from the river I love, and I once listened to an elder who recalls an elder saying to her people, when she was very young, that one day people would have to pay money for water to drink, and she, as a very young child, thought this idea was absurd, because, even then, clean water was so plentiful and so accessible that the idea of paying for water was laughable. But a lot can happen in one hundred and fifty years, and one hundred and fifty years from now, the glacial tongue of the Vatnajökull that I heard cracking like thunder late one afternoon as I sat at Sjónarnípa looking down, a glacial tongue which is, itself, more than 500 meters thick at some points, will have melted entirely away. One can already see how far it has receded—the mounds of earth it pushed before retreating are still there. Thirty years ago it was much further out, seventy years ago, it was not even a tongue for all the tongues that are now independent were still joined together and surrounding the peaks—one small part of a glacier so massive that it buries mountains entirely and even volcanic eruptions aren't always enough to breach its surface.

But in one hundred and fifty years, my red blood cells will have burst, releasing the iron that was created when a star collapsed into a white dwarf (signaling the end of fusion and the onset of a supernova explosion), the calcium and phosphorus in my bones will already be nutrients in the soil, my flesh will have become food for the bacteria already living within and upon me (as they migrate out of my lungs and digestive system and into my tissues), and the helium part of me, older even than the iron in my blood, will have begun its drift back out into the Milky Way.

8

It used to be that the horror would overwhelm me. Increasingly, now, it is the wonder. I used to be aware of the great emptiness inside of me but, since Iceland, everything is overflowing and I, too, was with everything or, perhaps, I was everything. I don't know, because I was not, I was not empty, I was overflowing. I was the overflowing more than I was an "I" that was participating in the overflowing. I suppose one name for this might be ecstasy.

Now, it's not that the horror vanished. The glacier is still is dying and we struck a bird with our car as it came up off the road and we had nowhere else to turn. But, for a while, the horror was overwhelmed. And in that overwhelming what shifted inside of me was the realization that I could be at peace in and with the horror, too.

I wonder, did Reinhold Hanning, the ninety-four-year-old man recently convicted for his role in the S.S. as a guard at Auschwitz, come to a similar realization at some point? Did he learn contentment in the midst of the horror, did he learn to journey to the wonder and experience the overflowing? During his trial he made the following statement, "I want to say that it disturbs me deeply that I was part of such a criminal organization. I am ashamed that I saw injustice and never did anything about it and I apologize for my actions. I am very, very sorry." And while people wring their hands and talk in puzzled tones, wondering how a person could ever, ever, ever do such a thing, I think of Cindy Gladue and Reuben Fox and Joseph Commanda and Blanche Hill-Easton and the boy with puss in his eyes and Tina Fontaine and Loretta Saunders and Dawn Crey and Joey English and Rowena Sharpe and Deidre Michelin and Ila Oman and Jeanenne Fontaine and Marilyn Munroe and Alannah Cardinal and Christine Cardinal and Annie Pootoogook and Brenda Campbell and Caitlin Potts and Azraya Ackabee-Kokopenace and Delaine Copenace and Charnelle Masakeyash and Victoria Crow Shoe and Gloria Gladue and Baby Girl and Brooklyn

A Magnificent Work

Moose and Delores Brown and Nadine Machiskinic and Krystal Andrews and Nellie Angutiguluk and Misty Potts and Kathleen Leary and Teresa Robinson and Beatrice Adam and Sindy Ruperthouse and Angela Poorman and Pamela Napoleon and Freda Goodrunning and Rocelyn Gabriel and Brandy Vittrekwa and Kelly Goforth and Cheyenne Fox and Richelle Bear and Samantha Paul and Immaculate Basil and Destiny Tom and Bella Laboucan-McLean and Heather Ballantyne and Leah Anderson and Shelly Dene and Bernadine Quewazance and Brandy Wesaquate and Deanna Bellerose and Simone Sanderson and Tiffany Skye and Verna Simard and Desiree Oldwoman and Angeline Pete and Tanya Nepinak and Justine Cochrane and Roxanne Isadore and Jeanette Cardinal and Ashley Machiskinic and Karina Wolfe and Janice Desjarlais and Abigail Andrews and Leslie Talley and Mildred Flett and Angela Meyer and Amber Guiboche and Amber Tuccaro and Nicole Daniels and Shelley Anderson and Hillary Wilson and Roxanne Charlie and Michelle Hadwen and Judy Quill and Tanya Brooks and Geraldine Beardy and Cherisse Houle and Violet Heathen and Della Ootoova and Ruth Cocks and Patricia Quinn and Anne Peters and Annette Holywhiteman and Delena Lefthand Dixon and Carolyn Connolly and Maisy Odjick and Jennifer Catcheway and Claudette Osborne and Shannon Alexander and Donna Taylor and Bonnie Joseph and Crystal Saunders and Shirley Waquan and Emily Osmond and Lorilee Francis and Angel Carlick and Leanne Benwell and Fonassa Bruyere and Jeannette Chief and Danita Bigeagle and Jacqueline Crazybull and Chantelle Bushie and Brittany Bearspaw and Andria Meise and Bonnie Jack and Marie Lasas and Aielah Saric-Auger and Kelly Morrisseau and Jeanine St. Jean and Tiffany Morrison and Juanita Cardinal and Shirley Cletheroe and Glennis Edwards and Sarah Obed and Heaven Traverse and Rose Decoteau and Delores Brower and Belinda Cameron and Jarita Naistus and Melanie Geddes and Rene Gunning and Melissa Chaboyer and Tamara Chipman and Krystle Knott and Marcia Koostachin and Sharon Abraham and Gladys Simon and Rhonda Gardiner and Janine Wesaquate and Elaine Alook and Maggie Burke and Rachel Quinney and Thelma Pete and Diana Rattlesnake and Cheryl Black and Tamra Keepness and Eva Mitchell and Cynthia Audy and Sunshine Wood and Pamela Holopainen and Moira Erb and Rena Fox and Katie Ballantyne and Felicia Solomon and Sylvia Guiboche and Nicolle Hands and Ramona Shular and Danielle LaRue and Lisa Young and Donna Kasyon and Maxine Wapass and Therena Silva and Edna Bernard and Tabitha Kalluk and Terrie Dauphinais and Angela Williams and Cheryl

The Fourth Part: Land

Johnson and Gladys Tolley and Carol Prudhomme and Roberta Elders and Savannah Hall and Audrey Desjarlais and Irma Murdock and Linda Scott and Mary Smith and Gloria Black Plume and Lora Banman and Elizabeth Dorion and Amanda Simpson and Michelle Gurney and Tania Marsden and Trudy Gopher and Ruby Hardy and Kellie Little and Marie Laliberte and Joyce Hewitt and Cassandra Antone and Janet Henry and Jessica Cardinal and Caralyn King and Kari Gordon and Loretta Capot-Blanc and Deborah Sloss and Olivia Williams and Diane Stewart and Amanda Cook and Joanne Ghostkeeper and Amanda Bartlett and Monica Jack and Dorothy Spence and Mary Lidguerre and Helen Gillings and Evaline Cameron and Rhonda Running Bird and Diane Dobson and Sarah Skunk and Lana Derrick and Janet Sylvestre and Alisha Germaine and Roxanne Thiara and Sonya Cywink and Jamie McGuire and Ramona Wilson and Marjorie Henderson and Sharon Merasty and Lora Frank and Monica Cardinal and Mary Goodfellow and Victoria Hornbrook and Roberta Lincoln and Joyce Tillotson and Patricia Carpenter and Sandra Johnson and Rose-Anne Blackned and Viola Panacheese and Lavina Tocher and Mariella Lennie and Shirley Lonethunder and Elsie Sebastian and Emily Ballantyne and Glenda Morrisseau and Mary Keadjuk and Delphine Nikal and Mavis Mason and Charlene Catholique and Cecilia Nikal and Doreen Jack and Terese Labbe and Wendy Poole and Leona Brule and Alberta Williams and Ernestine Kasyon and Barbara Shapwaykeesic and Bernadette Ahenakew and Debbie Pelletier and Margaret Vedan and Judy Chescue and Betsy Owens and Roberta Ferguson and Lindo Condo and Bernice Bottle and Carol Davis and Delores Whiteman and Mary Kreiser and Naomi Desjarlais and Maggie Mink and Cheryl Duck and Nancy Dumas and Mary Ann Birmingham and Marie Desjarlais and Darlinda Ritchey and Corrine Mossomin and Martha Boyce and Lori Berens and Jeanette Basil and Constance Cameron and Jane Sutherland and Marlene Abigosis and Patricia Favel and Edna Smith and Rebecca Guno and Marie Banks and Dawn Keewatin and Henrietta Millek and Roxanne Fleming and Barbara Keam and Myrna Montgrand and Mary Hill and Josephine Chakasim and Evelyn Kebalo and Mary Mark and Patricia Wadhams and Belinda Williams and Shirley Beardy and Lori Kasprick and Maggie Natomagan and Alice Netemegesic and Pauline Brazeau and Annie Yassie and Susan Assin and Carline Burns and Velma Duncan and Selina Wallace and Stella St. Arnault and Helene Ratfat and Jean Sampare and Geraldine Settee and Gloria Moody and Mabel Leo and Christina Littlejohn and Philomene Lemay and Jane Bernard and Doreen Hardy

A Magnificent Work

and Margaret Guylee and Emma Dixon and Marie Mike and Mae Morton and Jean Moccasin and Flora Muskego and Cecilia Payash and Margaret Blackbird and Linda Guimond and Marilyn Daniels and Frances Ellah and Serenity and Tanya Hill and Ada Brown and Sabrina Polchies and Harrison Burning and Isaiah Antone and Roy Wilson and Jesse Debo and Frank Winnie and Mildred Horne and Gary Ronald Hill and Marion Rebecca Hill and Carolyn Ann Jacobs and Lorne Gibson and Milford Gibson and Barbara Louise Hill and Pauline Joan Henry and Lorna and her sister No. 63, and No. 1296, 1309, 1313, 01307, 10317, 10334, 01342, 01360, 01185, 01224, 012363, 01272, 01275, 01341, 01343, 01284, and think, perhaps it is best if we, citizens of Canada, memorize these lines so we, too, can find words to express our remorse if we ever stand before the Court.

In Iceland, contentment burst upon me.
(I want to say . . .)
And it felt good.
(. . . that it disturbs me deeply . . .)
And I knew that I wanted to continue to feel that way.
(. . . that I was part of such a criminal organization . . .)
Content, even here, even now, in this world into which I have been thrown, and content to be content.
(. . . I am ashamed that I saw injustice . . .)
And there are some books I don't think I'll get around to reading now and I don't think I'll manage to finish the last seven hours of Claude Lanzmann's *Shoah* (1985). I thought maybe I could handle twenty minutes of the Holocaust per day but even that proved too much for me.
(. . . and never did anything about it . . .)
Because I want to continue to be content.
(. . . and I apologize for my actions . . .)
There is horror and there are mountains and I am content.
(. . . I am very, very sorry.)
I belong in the earth.

9

WHITE SUPREMACY HAS ALWAYS had a strong presence in my home town. The Klan came here very early in the 1920s and they never really left. They've rebranded in different ways, and tried to move into the public through various scenes. In the '80s they rallied around the so-called race science of a local professor. In the '90s, they resurfaced in the neo-Nazi movement that tried (and failed) to take over the local punk scene. Today, they are showing up again various patriotic, alt-right, Conservative, nationalist groups—from PEGIDA, to the Proud Boys, to the Soldiers of Odin, to the Three Percenters, to the Canadian variation of the Yellow Vest Movement. Not too long goes before they are rallying again in front of City Hall with Canadian flags and British flags and signs proclaiming that they totally can't be Nazis since they love the contemporary Israeli example of a militarized, colonial ethno-State.

It is notable that the increasingly popular and public transnational resurgence of fascism within these groups has been accompanied by appeals to "blood and soil" and claims of ancestral attachments to the land. Hence, getting "back to the land" and relearning the survival skills of rugged frontiersmen has been an essential component of the movements that launched the alt-Right and it continues to have a prominent place in various neo-fascist groups operating quite publicly today.

However, proclaiming the importance of one's attachment to the land is not the exclusive domain of Nazi-hipsters or soldiers in the Aryan Nations militia. The claim of belonging to a certain place, of being attached to the land where one lives, is fundamental to the construction of citizenship within settler colonial States. Thus, for example, the Canadian national anthem begins with these words:

A Magnificent Work

O Canada!
Our home and native land!
True patriot love in all thy sons command.

And, as a child, I remember singing a popular folk song that explicitly stated that this land is my land and that, in fact, this land was made for me and my people.

And what do I regularly hear proud Canadians praising about Canada in this sesquicentennial year of the Canadian occupation of these territories? How beautiful Canada's mountains are. The abundance of Canadian rivers and lakes. The ruggedness of the Canadian wilderness. And so on. This land is ours; this land is our home; this land is our native land. Of course, such thinking is dependent upon the myth of terra nullius and the erasure or extermination of Indigenous peoples and Indigenous sovereignties—leading to the inescapable conclusion that Canada simply cannot exist without missing and murdered Indigenous women—but much of this has been challenged in increasingly public ways over the last one hundred and fifty years. The Truth and Reconciliation Commission finally managed to expose the Canadian public to a fraction of the violence upon which its existence is premised and it did so with enough effort over enough time that the subject simply could not be avoided and ignored (ultimately forcing the federal government to initiate a National Inquiry into Missing and Murdered Indigenous Women and Girls, although the unfolding of that Inquiry has been an unmitigated disaster as the government has been sure to undercut, co-opt and redirect the commission so that it would not cause any harm to the government itself or its agents). However, much like white American citizens have responded to the Black Lives Matter movement (which has had a similar impact upon their collective consciousness) not with white penance but with a "white rage" that doubles down on institutional racism and a ruthlessly violent white supremacy, Canadians have responded by doubling down on their vision of Canada's greatness and their celebration of Canada's past and present.[1] As a result, new groups form and bring out old flags emphasizing Canada's connection to England, traditional Canadian values are celebrated and vehemently reasserted, smarmy, in your face, flag-waving patriotism becomes increasingly common, and the claim is repeatedly made that this land belongs to us. In all of this, I can no longer meaningfully distinguish between the patriotism of settlers occupying stolen lands and the nationalism of fascists calling for a white homeland.

1. On "white rage" see Anderson, *White Rage*.

The Fourth Part: Land

I think Kate Manne's analysis of the logic of misogyny helps to explain the lines of connection here. In her work, she carefully distinguishes between three things: patriarchy, misogyny, and sexism. Patriarchy is any context or social order in which men are favored over all others. Misogyny is "the "law enforcement" branch of patriarchal order, which has the overall function of *policing* and *enforcing* its governing ideology," and sexism, then, is "the "justificatory" branch of a patriarchal order, which consists in ideology that has the overall function of *rationalizing* and *justifying* patriarchal social relations."[2] Thus, as Manne goes on to say, sexism primarily discriminates between men and women and misogyny differentiates between good women and bad women (in order to punish the latter).[3] Changing her terms, while keeping an eye on these three definitions, is helpful for understanding the relationship between fascism and Canadian patriotism. For "patriarchy" we can substitute the context of settler colonialism, for "misogyny" we can substitute fascism, and for "sexism" we can substitute racism. We can, then, hypothesize that settler colonialism as a way of structuring life together on stolen land that is premised upon the extermination of Indigenous life. Fascism is the "law enforcement" branch of settler colonialism (distinguishing between "good Indians" who are willing to die, assimilate, or reconcile, and "bad Indians" who neither die nor assimilate, nor reconcile), and racism is the "justificatory" branch that rationalizes settler colonialism (distinguishing between occupiers and Indigenous peoples in a way similar to how patriarchy's sexism distinguishes between men and women). Consequently, just as Manne's logic leads to the conclusion that misogyny is a fundamental component of patriarchy, and not a random aberration that arises seemingly ex nihilo in mentally ill people, so also fascism is not an aberration within a settler colonial context but is, in fact, necessary for the ongoing existence of settler colonial States.

Walther Darré, who became Hitler's Reichsminister für Ernährung und Landwirtschaft, first developed the theory of blood and soil out of the teachings of his mentor, Karl Haushofer. He argued that the German people had a longstanding relationship and connection with the land of Germany (thus, as Anna Bramwell explains, "blood and soil" describes "the link between those who held and farmed the land and whose generations of blood, sweat and tears had made the soil part of their being, and their being integral to the soil") and he made this argument over and against the Jewish

---

2. Manne, *Down Girl*, 63, 79.
3. Manne, *Down Girl*, 80.

people who were said to be "wanderers" and "weeds" who did not belong and who, ultimately, were selected for extermination.[4] According to Darré, only Germans could own the land . . . but the land within Germany wasn't enough for them and so Poland had to be liberated and decolonized and restored to its rightful owners, and so on throughout Europe.

I was struck by how the discourse of blood and soil, mimics the ways in which Indigenous peoples talk about their belonging to this land. However, over against Nazis and neo-fascists who use their histories within certain lands to engage in genocidal and other forms of violence against outsider groups, Indigenous elders and land defenders in the territories occupied by Canada are not calling for the extermination of myself, my children, or my fellow Canadians. Despite all we have done, I regularly hear even the most militant Indigenous land defenders say that, if we learn to engage in relationships that are not premised upon violence and death, there is room for all of us. If we do not tear up the soil, if we do not poison the water, if we do not cut down the forests, if we do not dam the rivers, the land is big enough for us all. Where treaties were made, we simply need to honor the treaties (and honor *how Indigenous people understood those treaties*), we need to recognize Indigenous sovereignties, we need to stop stealing, we need to stop lying, and we need to finally, for once and for all, stop dressing up genocide and assimilation like friendship, care, and reconciliation.[5] Unlike fascists and neo-fascists, Indigenous peoples aren't calling for the death or disappearance of other peoples—they are saying that other peoples need to stop killing them. In order to do this, it may be necessary for Canada to stop existing, just as Rhodesia stopped existing and the Congo is no longer Belgian, but this doesn't mean that people who currently live as Canadians need to stop existing. In fact, colonizers may discover that their liberation is also only possible through the process of decolonization.

---

4. See Bramwell, *Blood and Soil*, 54; and throughout. But, nota bene, Bramwell writes as an apologist defending Darré! Therefore, it is important to read her work in light of responses like J. Sakai's "The Green Nazi: An Investigation into Fascist Ecology"; available online: http://readsettlers.org/green-nazi/text.html. Alexander Reid Ross also does a good job of exploring connections between fascism and environmentalism in *Against the Fascist Creep*.

5. As has now become clear, the Canadian government not only misrepresented the content of the written treaties to the various Indigenous peoples with whom they negotiated, but they also have consistently (up until the present day) misrepresented what Indigenous peoples agreed to when talking about these things with the Canadian public. See, for example, Krasowski, *No Surrender*.

The Fourth Part: Land

It is interesting then that White nationalists, partially in response to an increasing awareness related to Canada's ongoing history of genocide, have pushed an eco-conscious back to the land ideology that often emphasizes the sacredness of nature emphasizes the beauty and wonder and significance of plant and animal life. When I first became aware of this, I felt unsettled and concerned that I may have committed some kind of fundamental error in my own thinking. Because, here I am, a settler occupying stolen land, trying to find my way and I, too, have been increasingly valuing a sense of attachment to the land and the richness and value and beauty of all forms of life. This concern only deepened when I realized that some fascist groups were intimately connected with neo-tribalism and neo-paganism. The discourse of these groups has striking parallels to the words of some Indigenous people whom I highly respect, who have also called Canadians who occupy these territories to go back to rediscover their pre-Roman, pre-Christian indigenous identities in order to learn how to engage in decolonization and in order to relearn a proper relationship with the land. Initially, I felt quite disoriented by these parallels. How can it be, I asked myself, that those most committed to the genocide accompanying colonization can sound like those most committed to decolonization?

However, apart from the very obvious death-dealing white supremacy (often cloaked in pseudo-science or warped social science), that defines the fascists over against Indigenous peoples who consistently talk about the value of all peoples, there are other absolutely crucial differences. The first is the difference between claiming to own or possess a land, upon which we then impose our cultures, and claiming that we belong to the land and that the land gives us our cultures. In the first approach, the land is transformed into property (and "natural resources" which are then exploited to produce wealth) and in the second approach it is the land that informs people about what kinds of relationships they are to have with everything that constitutes "the land" (from the soil to the forests to the plants to the animals to the water to the air to other people—all of these constitute the land). Thus, fascism is based upon white possessiveness, or, perhaps better stated, the legalization of White theft, whereas Indigenous approaches are rooted in a sense of interconnectedness and respect, wherein people function as caretakers of the land to ensure that it remains in the state in which it was received for subsequent generations.[6]

---

6. On White possessiveness and White theft, see Moreton-Robinson, *The White Possessive*; and Nichols, *Theft is Property!*.

A Magnificent Work

In this regard, it seems to me that both fascism and Indigenous perspectives recognize a seemingly universal desire for belonging, but fascism substitutes ownership and lordship—a hierarchy of the ruler and the ruled, the owner and the owned—for the Indigenous view of interwoven relationships of mutual care and responsibility. Fascism says, this is my home because it belongs to me. Indigenous voices say, this is my home because I belong here. It is the difference between belongings and belonging (words that might look similar to the uninformed but which bear very different meanings). However, it seems to me that, despite its best efforts, the history of capitalism has shown us that belongings can never actually replace a sense of belonging. That's why white people need to always steal more—maybe I will finally and fully feel at home if I own everything, maybe I will finally and fully feel at home if nobody else is left. But grabbing more will never satisfy this desire and so this thieving possessiveness, this transformation of interconnectedness into ownership, propels a death drive. As Alanis Obomsawin says:

> Canada, the most affluent of countries, operates on a depletion economy which leaves destruction in its wake. Your people are driven by a terrible sense of deficiency. When the last tree is cut, the last fish is caught, and the last river is polluted; when to breathe the air is sickening, you will realize, too late, that wealth is not in bank accounts and that you can't eat money.[7]

The end result of this isn't a homeland (or, if you prefer the German, a Heimat), it's a wasteland where a space-time-matter once overflowing with life is finally transformed into what the colonizers claimed it always was—terra nullius. At this point, the occupiers, like a locust swarm, must either die or move on.

A further critical difference between fascism and Indigenous perspectives follows from this. How one understands owning and belonging-to also seems to set the standard for how relationships between men and women are understood. Fascism, in past and present forms, is dominated by men who fetishize violence. Hence, the current rise of fascist groups parallels a rise of more explicitly and openly misogynistic Men's Rights Activist groups (which then become recruiting grounds for more explicitly fascist organizers).[8] From their perspective, women are akin to the land—they are considered the property of men. In fact, as Sylvia Federici has shown, the

---

7. Quoted in Poole, "Conversations with North American Indians," 43.
8. For a background on some of these men see Kimmel, *Angry White Men*.

counter-revolutionary unification of classes necessary to the rise of capitalism was accomplished by replacing common lands with common women—i.e. by privatizing the commons while making women the property of men (and women who resisted this were classified as witches and murdered).[9] Further, given the way in which witch-hunts transcended Catholic and Protestant divides (most often being enforced by secular rather than religious courts), Federici argues that this war on women was the first truly unifying terrain of the European Nation-States that emerged alongside of capitalism. Then, as capitalism develops, white supremacy becomes an increasingly useful component of it. As Nell Irvin Painter demonstrates, the category of Whiteness was continually modified and expanded to include the Irish, Eastern Europeans, or Europeans from the Mediterranean coast, in order to maintain structures of slavery and colonization that were premised upon the death or bondage of Indigenous people, black people, and other people of color.[10] Fascism becomes a useful tool for maintaining this counter-revolutionary, class-transcending racial solidarity and so some scholars argue that the first fascist group was actually the Ku Klux Klan that formed in America in 1866 during the so-called "Reconstruction" of the postbellum South. Thus, patriarchy is deeply integrated with colonization and European statecraft. The white homeland is also the Fatherland ("this is my Father's world, oh let me ne'er forget . . ."), defended not by patriotic children but by patriotic sons. Women become the property of men, useful to the extent that they are able to reproduce the white race, maintain an adequate population of workers, and produce male heirs. Hence, Walther Darré's vision of England after it has been conquered by Nazi Germany:

> The old and weak will be exterminated. All men remaining in Britain as slaves will be sterilised; a million or two of the young women of the Nordic type will be segregated in a number of stud farms where, with the assistance of picked German sires, during a period of 10 or 12 years, they will produce annually a series of Nordic infants to be brought up in every way as Germans.[11]

On the other hand, Indigenous peoples, from the Mi'kmaq on the Eastern shore of Turtle Island to the Sto:lo on the Western coast, also understand women in connection to the land but the connection made here is

9. See Federici, *Caliban and the Witch*.

10. See Painter, *The History of White People*. See also Allen, *The Invention of the White Race* (2 vols.).

11. Quoted here: http://www.holocaustresearchproject.org/economics/darre.html.

based on parallel powers of creation and the ability to give life. Thus, when Isapo-Muxika from the Siksika Nation said, "As long as the sun shines and the waters flow, this land will be here to give life to men and animals," the life-giving water that he references is not only the water found in lakes and rivers but, also, the water that flows from a woman's body during childbirth. As a result of this, men no more own the women than they own the land. In fact, men are regularly structurally subordinated to women with many nations being matrilineal, with men leaving their clans and nations to join the clans and nations of the women who choose to marry them, and with male warriors and chiefs being accountable to female elders (hence, when Canada gained its independence from Britain and begin its sustained assault upon Indigenous modes of structuring life together, the Indian Act forced a patriarchal structure onto Indigenous politics in order to enforce assimilation). This is the mode of being in relationship with one another that the land has taught people across Turtle Island. It is life-affirming and values that which is life-giving. You need a European to imagine that something like a death drive could be a universal human characteristic.

It has sometimes been argued that evil thrives, not because it is purely evil, but because it takes something good and corrupts, twists, or perverts it. From this perspective, great evils can often be perversions of great goods. This, I think, explains the ways in which fascist voices mimic voices of liberation. But it is only White people, especially White men, who are fooled by this.

10

THERE IS A BIOELECTROGENIC fish common to the Mediterranean and Black Seas who buries most of itself in the sand and dirt on the sea floor. It is called a Stargazer because its enlarged eyes, which remain unburied, are continually staring into the firmament above. It looks like something out of a child's nightmare or like a monster from an 8-bit dungeon crawler designed for the Atari—a skull with bulging eyes and a gaping mouth full of jagged teeth. Since seeing it, I have a gained a new perspective on myself when I, full of awe, full of wonder, a skull with bulging eyes and a gaping mouth full of jagged teeth, stare up into the heavens.

11

NICHE CONSTRUCTION IS A process by which organisms engage in a feedback loop with their environment and, thereby, influence the ways in which they evolve—i.e. it is one of the ways in which organisms are active agents in their own evolution.[1] Via niche construction, organisms craft environments that are a better fit for them, while also then evolving in ways to better fit that environment (this, along with the stream of evolutionary theory that emphasizes the role of mutual aid in the survival of species, is one of the areas of research that problematizes the overly simplistic Darwinian or neo-Darwinian models of evolution).

For example, as Peter Wohlleben has shown, most trees prefer to spend their lives living with other trees, in part, because a forest creates an ideal microclimate for them and permits them to live longer, healthier lives.[2] Forests shield trees from strong winds, reduce both extreme heat and extreme cold, and permit the storage of large amounts of water. Furthermore, rich, dense, and incredibly intricate fungal networks develop in the forest floor and allows trees to send messages and food to each other and, while trees tend to only want to support their own species, the fungi values diversity and will often redistribute food not on the basis of species but on the basis of need. This kind of sharing can even extend to stumps and scientists have discovered stumps that have been able to continue to live for hundreds of years because they were receiving food supplies from other trees through their roots—not only this but a spruce tree was discovered with roots that were 9,550 years old because successive trees had grown up atop the stump of the prior tree and the original root system had remained alive and attached to each tree. This care does not only extent to one's immediate neighbors but can be used in the process of constructing

1. See Sultan, *Organism and Environment*.
2. *The Hidden Life of Trees*.

the forest as a whole. Thus, with the aid of these fungal networks, the trees in undisturbed beech forests have been shown to photosynthesize at the same rate, meaning that all the trees will grow at the same rate and thickness, regardless of whether or not they are located at an advantageous or disadvantageous microsite.

Trees rely upon this mutual aid because the odds are that each fully grown tree, regardless of the number of seeds it produces (and, over the course of a lifetime spanning centuries, many trees can produce significantly more than a million seeds), will only end up producing one offspring that will grow to full size. Most trees, in other word, evolve to live best in forests but forests are one way in which trees go about engaging in niche construction and building a world that is suited to their needs (although forests, themselves, can be understood as an organism—a superorganism like an ant colony—leading again to the question of where one form of life ends and where another begins and where we draw the lines between what is "organism" and what is "environment"). When trees create forests, they also contribute to the flourishing of a multitude of other forms of life. This takes place in the forest as a whole, but also in each individual tree.

And the same thing is happening all around us in all lifeforms. Thus, for example, as much as I engage in niche construction, the bacteria in my digestive tract, in my lungs, in my brain, and on my skin are also doing the same (and continually communicating with each other as they do so). Bacteria are constantly shaping the organisms that host them, just as the organisms that host them also shape those bacteria.

Plants or animals that engage in niche construction in a manner the leads to diversification and the proliferation of a various life forms have been labeled "ecosystem engineers." The most cited example of this kind of creature is probably Ahmik, the North American Beaver, Castor Canadensis, whose dam building creates dramatic changes within ecosystems and draws in a very rich and diverse spectrum of other living things. But focusing on the beaver can be misleading. Predators can also be ecosystem engineers by maintaining a balance between numerous species that compete for the same resources. The removal of a predatory starfish from an ecosystem resulted in the number of other flourishing species to drop from fifteen to eight. And restoring wolves to Yellowstone caused a massive explosion of biodiversity—resulting, even, in healthier rivers—that had been almost entirely destroyed by rampant elk populations. In fact, it has been proposed the vertebrates have more complicated immune systems than invertebrates,

A Magnificent Work

because vertebrates have co-evolved with many more species of bacteria living within and upon their bodies. The cells of the immune systems function in a manner similar to predators like starfish or wolves, preventing a single species from outcompeting others, engaging in ecosystem engineering and a form of niche construction that ensures a richer and healthier diversity of species. But this engineering goes both ways—it is highly probable that the development of immune systems, at least within mammals, is a process in which bacteria participate.[3] Remove certain bacteria, and the organism is immunocompromised. Restore the bacteria to the host, and the immune system recovers and develops in a healthier manner. Thus, while our immune system engages in niche construction and ecosystem engineering with bacteria, the bacteria are doing the exact same thing, at the same time, with us and with the very tools we are using as we act.

The so-called advance of civilization, via an accelerating process containing at least three world-changing events (the Agricultural Revolution and the advent of civilization, the Industrial Revolution and the rise of the machine, and then the Digital Revolution and the spread of the world wide web), is one particular form of niche construction. Civilization-building is a form of niche construction by which we influence how we evolve as human beings. Viewed in this way, it raises the following questions: what kind of environment are we trying to create for ourselves, what does fitness to this environment look like, what sort of feedback loop does it create, and how does this effect other forms of life?[4] I think the answers to all these questions are troubling.

It appears that we are trying to create an environment from which we have separated ourselves in order to attain mastery over it. We demonstrate and attain this separation and mastery by destroying the environment—but then the more we destroy the environment, the more our separation from it becomes necessary and so a destructive feedback loop occurs that has devastating consequences for many, many other forms of life. Ultimately, however, the suggestion that we are separate from our environment is an illusion. And it is a deadly illusion. Our version of niche construction is

---

3. See, for example, Demas and Nelson (eds.), *Ecoimmunology*; and the chapters found in Part IV of Ngai, Henderson and Ruby (eds.), *The Influence of Cooperative Bacteria on Animal Host Biology*.

4. It was *Eating the Sun*, Oliver Morton's exceptionally beautiful and wide-ranging study of life and earth (disguised as a study of photosynthesis), that first got me thinking seriously about feedback loops. I have found that this theme has become ever more central to my own thinking and organizing over the years.

one of accelerating mutually assured destruction. Civilization is a snake eating its own tail, it's an oil pipe leaking in Sioux territory, it's the Unit Two reactor core from Fukushima that it took scientists six years to even locate.

Here, again, I think of Peter Maurin's wisdom when he suggested that we need to make the kind of society where it is easier for people to be good (ecological developmental biologists would be impressed by his insights, coming as they did well before their field of research had been created). We need to engage in a form of niche construction wherein fitness to our environment is premised upon contributing to that which is life-giving and life-affirming, wherein integration is premised upon mutual trust and mutual care—not just between individual people or communities but between species and ecosystems—and where we create a feedback loop that encourages the thriving of all life within the environment, rather than sustaining one that is premised upon the destruction of, well, almost everything. Not only listening to but also following teachings Indigenous to the land where one lives is one way to start into this journey.

Kindness is a second way.

At the core of kindness is treating others in a way that makes them feel special. The inherent specialness of ourselves and others and all of life, is what used to be contained in the notion of the sacred. The rapaciousness of my people has been enabled by the cordoning off of sacredness, reserving it for an especially small number of people or things—forests that are not sacred can be logged, lakes that are not sacred can be drained, mountains that are not sacred can be mined, buffalo that are not sacred can be stampeded, en masse, over cliffs, and people that are not sacred can be exploited, ignored, starved, murdered, or disappeared—until sacredness itself is gone. But without sacredness, people lose their sense of specialness—they want to believe in it, they long for it, but they don't know where they can find a basis for it and, besides, so many other voices are telling them the opposite.

But when people don't feel special, they will settle for feeling superior and think that it amounts to the same thing. But it doesn't. Recognizing that a specific person is special doesn't require us to see other people as not special; but recognizing that a specific person is superior requires us, at least in some way, to see other people as inferior. Specialness thrives in the context of being together with others in relationships of mutual wonder, curiosity, respect, and honor. Superiority thrives in the context of hierarchical relationships when we approach others as competitors, stepping stones, and fodder for our own egos.

A Magnificent Work

And teaching specialness doesn't mean we don't teach other things—as if teaching a young White boy and a young White girl that they are special means that I somehow can't teach that boy and girl about White privilege, patriarchal violence, heteronormativity, and the racist and colonial structures that shape our life together. Because, if we are to go about teaching specialness, we must never stop emphasizing the specialness of those who are most oppressed, most alone, most abused, and most targeted by the men and structures of nations of violence (and part of teaching specialness means working to change those things). And so, my darlings, yes, you are special. You are so special that thinking about your specialness makes me weep tears of joy and wonder and gratitude. And, yes, my darlings, you, in all your specialness, are intimately connected with and responsible to others who are just as special.

Isn't that amazing?

(My god, what a beautiful picture. Thank you! It's perfect, I love it—can I have another?)

12

PEGIDA WAS HOLDING ANOTHER rally in front of City Hall and so I danced with my daughter at the Rally Against Hate, my son on my shoulders, laughing and singing. I am a father and I am accountable to these children just as we, together, are accountable to others. The daylight—neither more nor less than both a particle and a wave—also danced and we, too, along with everything else, are both particles and waves. We are in the everything and the everything is in us, and together our voices and bodies vibrated with songs of love. We vibrated as everything has and does and always will do.

My father took from me because he believed those who said they took his specialness. But they lied. Specialness is not a thing that can be taken. My father took from me, but he did not take my specialness. My father took from me, but he did not take my fatherliness. My father took from me, but he did not take my interconnectedness. My father took from me, but the everything remains. My father took from me but, still, I belong. I belong with these children. I belong in the everything. I belong in the earth.

Nii'kinaaganaa. All my relations.

Bibliography

Allen, Theodore W. *The Invention of the White Race*. 2 Volumes. London: Verso, 2012.
Anderson, Carol. *White Rage: The Unspoken Truth of Our Racial Divide*. New York: Bloomsbury, 2017.
Anderson, Kim, Maria Campbell and Christi Belcourt. *Keetsahnak / Our Missing and Murdered Indigenous Sisters* edited by Kim Anderson, Maria Campbell, and Christi Belcourt. Edmonton: University of Alberta, 2018.
Anderson, Mark Cronlund and Carmen L. Robertson. *Seeing Red: A History of Natives in Canadian Newspapers*. Winnipeg: University of Manitoba Press, 2011.
Archibald, John. *One Plus One Equals One: Symbiosis and the Evolution of Complex Life*. Oxford: Clarendon, 2014.
Bramwell, Anna. *Blood and Soil: Walter Darré and Hitler's Green Party*. Windsor: Kensal Press, 1985.
Céline, Louis-Ferdinand. *Journey to the End of the Night*. Translated by Ralph Mannheim. Introduction by William T. Vollmann. New York: New Directions, 1988.
Cordingley, Michael C. *Viruses: Agents of Evolutionary Invention*. Cambridge: Harvard University, 2017.
Davies, Paul. *The Eerie Silence: Searching for Ourselves in the Universe*. New York: Penguin, 2011.
Demas, Gregory E. and Randy J. Nelson. *Ecoimmunology*. Oxford: Oxford University, 2012.
DeSalle, Rob and Susan L. Perkins. *Welcome to the Microbiome: Getting to Know the Trillions of Bacteria and Other Microbes In, On, and Around You*. Illustrated by Patricia J. Wynne. New Haven: Yale University, 2015.
Federici, Sylvia. *Caliban and the Witch: Women, the Body and Primitive Accumulation*. New York: Autonomedia, 2004.
Fournier, Suzanne and Ernie Crey. *Stolen From Our Embrace: The Abduction of First Nations Children and the Restoration of Aboriginal Communities*. Photographs by David Neil. Vancouver: Douglas and MacIntyre, 1997.
Frankl, Viktor E. *Man's Search for Meaning: An Introduction to Logotherapy*. Boston: Beacon, 1963.
Golubic, Stjepko. "Microbial Mats of Abu Dhabi" in *Environmental Evolution: Effects of the Origin and Evolution of Life on Planet Earth*. Edited by Lynn Margulis and Lorraine Olendzenski. Third Printing (Cambridge: MIT, 1999): 103–30.

Bibliography

———. "Stromatolites of Shark Bay" in *Environmental Evolution: Effects of the Origin and Evolution of Life on Planet Earth*. Edited by Lynn Margulis and Lorraine Olendzenski. Third Printing (Cambridge: MIT, 1999): 131–47.
Government of Canada. National Centre for Truth and Reconciliation, University of Manitoba. *Mohawk Indian Residential School IAP School Narrative*. May 2013. Accessed February 28, 2017.
Graeber, David. *Bullshit Jobs: A Theory*. New York: Simon & Schuster, 2018.
Graham, Elizabeth. *The Mush Hole: Life at Two Indian Residential Schools*. Waterloo: Heffle Publishing, 1997.
Hitchin, Neil and the Governor and Court of the New England Company. *'Come Over and Help Us': The New England Company and Its Mission. 1649–2001*. Ely, Great Britain: St. Pancras Publishing and Research, 2002.
Hickman, Carole S. "How have bacteria contributed to the evolution of multicellular animals?" in *The Influence of Cooperative Bacteria on Animal Host Biology*. Advances in Molecular and Cellular Microbiology 10. Edited by Margaret McFall-Ngai, Brian Henderson and Edward G. Ruby (Cambridge: Cambridge University, 2005): 3–33.
hooks, bell. *The Will to Change: Men, Masculinity, and Love*. New York: Atria, 2004.
Jablonka, Eva and Marion J. Lamb. *Evolution in Four Dimensions: Genetic, Epigenetic, Behavioral, and Symbolic Variation in the History of Life*. Illustrated by Anna Zeligowski. Cambridge: MIT, 2014.
Karapanou, Margarita. *Kassandra and the Wolf*. Translated by N. C. Germanacos. Northampton MA: Clockroot, 2009.
Kimmel, Michael. *Angry White Men: American Masculinity at the End of an Era*. New York: Bold Type, 2017.
King, Barbara J. *How Animals Grieve*. Chicago: The University of Chicago, 2013.
Krasowski, Sheldon. *No Surrender: The Land Remains Indigenous*. Foreword by Winona Wheeler. Regina: University of Regina, 2019.
Levin, Peter A. *Trauma and Memory: Brain and Body in Search of a Living Past. A Practical Guide for Understanding and Working with Traumatic Memory*. Foreword by Bessel Van Der Kolk. Berkeley: North Atlantic Books, 2015.
Library and Archives of Canada. School File Series—1879–1953 (RG 10-B-3-d). Accessed March 11,2017. http://www.bac-lac.gc.ca/eng/discover/mass-digitized-archives/school-files-1879-1953/Pages/school-files-1879-1953.aspx.
Lux, Maureen K. *Separate Beds: A History of Indian Hospitals in Canada, 1920s—19080s*. Toronto: University of Toronto Press, 2016.
MacFarlane, Robert. *Landmarks*. London: Penguin Books, 2015.
Maltz, Wendy. *The Sexual Healing Journey: A Guide for Survivors of Sexual Abuse, Third Edition*. Newly revised and updated. New York: HarperCollins, 2012.
Manne, Kate. *Down Girl: The Logic of Misogyny*. Oxford: Oxford University, 2019.
Margulis, Lynn and Lorraine Olendzenski, Editors. *Environmental Evolution: Effects of the Origin and Evolution of Life on Planet Earth*. Third Printing. Cambridge: MIT, 1999.
Maté, Gabor. *When the Body Says No: The Cost of Hidden Stress*. Toronto: Vintage, 2003.
Maurin, Peter. *Easy Essays*. Catholic Worker Reprint Series. Eugene, OR: Wipf & Stock, 2010.
McCarthy, Cormac. *Blood Meridian: Or the Evening Redness of the Sun*. New York: Random House, 1985.
———. *The Border Trilogy: All the Pretty Horses, The Crossing, Cities of the Plain*, Everyman's Library. New York: Alfred A. Knopf, 1999.

Bibliography

McDiarmid, Jessica. *Highway of Tears: A True Story of Racism, Indifference, and the Pursuit of Justice for Missing and Murdered Indigenous Women and Girls.* Toronto: Doubleday, 2019.
McFall-Ngai, Margaret J., Briand Henderson and Edward G. Ruby, Editors. *The Influence of Cooperative Bacteria on Animal Host Biology.* Advances in Molecular and Cellular Microbiology 10. Cambridge: Cambridge University, 2005.
Metatawabin, Edmund with Alexanra Shimo. *Up Ghost River: A Chief's Journey Through the Turbulent Waters of Native History.* Toronto: Vintage, 2014.
Milloy, John S. *"A National Crime": The Canadian Residential School System. 1879 to 1986.* Critical Studies in Native History 11. Winnipeg: The University of Manitoba Press, 1999.
Moreton-Robinson, Aileen. *The White Possessive: Property, Power, and Indigenous Sovereignty.* Minneapolis: University of Minnesota, 2015.
Morrison, Toni. *Beloved.* New York: Vintage, 2004.
Morton, Oliver. *Eating the Sun: How Plants Power the Planet.* New York: Harper Perennial, 2009.
The National Inquiry into Missing and Murdered Indigenous Women and Girls. *Reclaiming Power and Place: The Final Report of the National Inquiry into Missing and Murdered Indigenous Women and Girls.* Available online here: https://www.mmiwg-ffada.ca/final-report/
Newsom, Jennifer Seibel. *The Mask You Live In.* San Francisco: The Representation Project, 2015.
Nichols, Robert. *Theft is Property! Dispossession and Critical Theory.* Durham, NC: Duke University, 2020.
Nouwen, Henri. *Life of the Beloved: Spiritual Living in a Secular World.* New York: Crossroad, 1992.
———. *The Wounded Healer: Ministry in Contemporary Society.* New York: Doubleday, 1972.
Osborne, Ralph, Editor. *Who is the Chairman of This Meeting?: A Collection of Essays.* Toronto: Neewin, 1972.
Painter, Nell Irvin. *The History of White People.* London: W. W. Norton, 2011
Poole, Ted. "Conversations with North American Indians" in *Who is the Chairman of This Meeting?: A Collection of Essays.* Edited by Ralph Osborne (Toronto: Neewin, 1972): 39–52.
Ross, Alexander Reid. *Against the Fascist Creep.* Chico, CA: AK, 2017.
Safina, Carl. *Beyond Words: What Animals Think and Feel.* New York: Picador, 2016.
Sebald, W. G. *Austerlitz.* Translated by Anthea Bell. Toronto: Vintage, 2001.
———. *The Emigrants.* Translated by Michael Hulse. London: Harvill, 1992.
———. *The Rings of Saturn.* Translated by Michael Hulse. London: Harvill, 1998.
Sangharakshita. *The Bodhisattva Ideal: Wisdom and Compassion in Buddhism.* Cambridge: Windhorse, 1999.
Starblanket, Tamar. *Suffer the Little Children: Genocide, Indigenous Nations and the Canadian State.* Foreword by Ward Churchill. Atlanta: Clarity, 2018.
Sultan, Sonia E. *Organism and Environment: Ecological Development, Niche Construction, and Adaptation.* Oxford: Oxford University, 2015.
Toews, Mariam. *A Complicated Kindness.* Toronto: Vintage, 2004.
Van Der Kolk, Bessel. *The Body Keeps the Score: Brain, Mind, and Body in the Healing of Trauma.* New York: Penguin, 2014.

Bibliography

Wohlleben, Peter. *The Hidden Life of Trees: How They Feel, What They Communicate—Discoveries from a Secret World*. Translated by Jane Billinghurst with a Foreword by Tim Flannery. Vancouver: Greystone, 2016.

Yong, Ed. *I Contain Multitudes: The Microbes Within Us and a Grander View of Life*. New York: Ecco, 2016.

Zimmer, Carl. *She Has Her Mother's Laugh: The Powers, Perversions, and Potential of Heredity*. New York: Dutton, 2018.

www.ingramcontent.com/pod-product-compliance
Lightning Source LLC
Chambersburg PA
CBHW072130160426
43197CB00012B/2051